Foreword

By Denis Canavan

On 18 September 2014, the people of Scotland will have a once-in-a-lifetime opportunity. They can choose a continuation of austerity under the UK, or they can choose a different path. Independence is not an end in itself. It is a means of empowering the people of Scotland to build a better Scotland, a more prosperous Scotland, a fairer Scotland.

Different people may have different visions of independence and how their vision can be turned into reality. The aptly named 'Moving On' puts forward a powerful case for prioritising the freedom of people, rather than the freedom of market forces. If the bankers and big business interests are left running the Scottish economy, then the people of Scotland will not be truly free or independent. Neo-liberal economic policies have widened the gap between rich and poor, and the failure of Westminster politicians to regulate the financial institutions has allowed bankers to bring us to the brink of economic ruin.

Independence should not mean a continuation of the same failed policies which have made the UK the fourth most unequal society in the developed world. Independence is an opportunity for a fresh start and that means fresh thinking. In that respect, Andy Anderson and Ronnie Morrison make a very valuable contribution to the current debate, drawing on important lessons from the past, and offering hope for a brighter future.

(Dennis Canavan is a former Independent MSP and Chairman Advisory Board of Yes Scotland, and The campaign for a Yes vote in the Scottish Independence Referendum.)

CONTENTS

PART TWO – Finding the Money

PREFACE

Referendum Day 2014 presents everyone over sixteen and resident in Scotland with an equal vote. We must decide if our country, after 300 years as part of the United Kingdom, will once again become a Self-governing Nation.

Considered without emotion, this is perhaps no big deal. Most nations, large and small the world over, have such a right. Indeed, they take it for granted.

It is, nevertheless, an important event for the people of Scotland. It will be the first time in their long and interesting history that they have been offered such a choice.

The past has been full of events relating to their struggles as a Nation, fighting for their freedom and independence from the Romans, the Vikings, the Normans, and from their southern neighbour England. Such struggles are at the very heart of our history and culture.

So this Referendum is a credit to both the people of Scotland and the United Kingdom. Seldom has a question of such fundamental import been decided by a simple majority vote and without the struggle, bloodshed and suffering experienced by so many countries seeking to break the domination of Westminster.

Unfortunately that does not mean that the run up to the vote is being conducted in a gentlemanly fashion. There are strong vested interests at the economic heart of this issue, and many will employ every means at their disposal to defend them, whilst claiming to benefit the community.

We have seen threats, warnings, ugly fears, confusion, misrepresentation, outright lies and distorted statistics being used to deter or frighten people away from independence, and these will persist until polling day.

The authors are determined that these interests must be exposed and prevented from undermining true independence.

Despite their different experiences, both take a similar view of the economic situation in Scotland and the UK. They see the need not only to regain political independence, but to return ultimate responsibility for the conduct of the economy and the banking system to full democratic accountability. They maintain that there can be no true independence without financial independence, and they are in complete agreement as to the means and policies which will achieve this.

Early media debate following the publication of the Scottish Government's White Paper has exposed a truly remarkable anomaly. The SNP are arguing to retain Sterling and the Bank of England; conversely the pro-union camp suggests an independent Scotland may not be allowed to join a Sterling Zone. To many of us it is incomprehensible that any newly independent country would wish to saddle itself with a money system which is so clearly unfit for purpose. Indeed without being released from Sterling few of the aspirations of the White Paper will be achievable.

Even from a negotiating point of view the SNP should have prepared a Plan B. Had they done so and enlisted some genuinely independent advice it would have been apparent which was Plan A and which Plan B. Just how this affects every issue in the White Paper and beyond will become clear as this remarkable story unfolds. No longer will you 'turn off' when you hear the BBC announce the latest deliberations of the Monetary Policy Committee, followed by some economists speculating upon the reaction of financial markets.

Now you will recognise the gobbledegook for what it is, propaganda from the City of London disseminated by the trusted BBC. The underlying message is that you may not understand this because monetary economics is a complicated subject, but rest assured the nation's affairs are in expert hands. Propaganda works only when it is not questioned.

Everyone deserves full access to the facts. The refusal of the UK government to accept the recommendation of the Electoral Commission, or to discuss issues openly with the Scottish government about agreed arrangements in the event of a yes vote, is unhelpful and undemocratic.

Such misrepresentations aside, most Scots accept that independence alone will not resolve all their daily problems, but they have every justification in seeking a lot more detail. Independence is far more than voting for the incumbent political personalities; it is for the long term, and that demands a well prepared strategy. Perhaps these pages will provide some food for thought.

The authors of this book come from very different backgrounds and have entirely different life experiences. Ronnie is an accountant by training. He is very much a self-made businessman who employed several hundred people in his innovative construction and manufacturing enterprises in both Scotland and England, as well as overseas. Andy by contrast left school at 15 to work in Blairhall colliery in Fife. He has been a soldier, a piper in the Cameron Highlanders, a coal miner, and an active trade-unionist.

He won a scholarship from the National Union of Mineworkers to study at Ruskin College Oxford, and later won a state scholarship to study politics, philosophy and economics at New College, Oxford. He then worked as a full-time official of the National Union of Public Employees until his retirement.

Sometimes Westminster may pursue an agenda which makes you feel uncomfortable. If so then you need to read this book. You will find an alternative which confirms that which you have long suspected. There are two varieties of economic and monetary policy – the kind that serves the 1% in the City of London, and the kind you can read about here which serves the other 99%. Your time will be well invested in examining this fresh approach to the economic and monetary policy of Independence.

The story is contained in two parts, combined here into one volume. Part One is written by Andy and looks at our economic history, from Adam Smith, Marx and Keynes to the present. This forms a foundation for a set of economic policies tailored to the priorities of an independent Scotland. In so doing it provides both the theory and the means to achieve and maintain full employment.

In Part Two, Ronnie looks at the financial options which flow from this, and, as will be seen, quickly concludes that Scotland will need its own currency. That in turn makes possible much overdue reform of the banking system and opens doors to a variety of alternative monetary policies.

This section is much more than a proposal for an independent currency; it is a complete tool-kit with a specific blueprint for its introduction and transition from sterling.

The two parts combine to present independence as an opportunity to rethink our priorities.

PART ONE

The Economic Ideas

PART ONE

INTRODUCTION

We recognise that the subject of economics and high finance are not considered among the most popular of topics, indeed we know they are usually boring. So we will make a special effort to confine ourselves to the essentials, and try to make the story as interesting as we can.

We are however, where we are today, not altogether by chance or evolution. Economic theories and myths continue to play significant roles; conscious political decisions are made, and economic pressures shape the way we live. We need to separate out the wheat from the chaff, the policies which serve the common weal, and those with a more narrow and selfish agenda. Only then can we demonstrate a credible means of redirecting our energies more responsibly and productively.

This is not an academic paper, and so we shall avoid peppering the narrative with footnotes, but our sources are mainly the Office of National Statistics, (ONS), or the Government Expenditure & Revenues Scotland, (GERS), or other government publications. Similarly, allusions to familiar texts in economic theory will not be referenced.

Where we have quoted from other writers however, we do provide full acknowledgement. (*See Bibliography*)

PART ONE

CHAPTER 1

Early Economists

Adam Smith

Our story begins in Glasgow, in the late 18th century, with a philosophy professor of Glasgow University, Adam Smith, and his book '*An Inquiry into the Nature and Causes of the Wealth of Nations*' (1776).

Adam Smith is considered the father of economics, and even today 237 years after the publication of his book, Adam Smith's ideas are still important, and are still respected all over the world. There is no other economist who would be accepted, respected, and studied as a fundamental part of economic theory in so many different parts of the world today; the USA, UK, China, Russia, India, indeed everywhere in the modern world.

Adam Smith's unique position in this respect is because he worked vigorously to understand and to explain his economic theory in a scientific way. He rejected the old mythology which surrounded this subject and attempted to examine it and analyse it objectively. This is what made him a leading figure in the 18th Century Scottish Enlightenment, and is undoubtedly the reason for the long-term strength of his ideas.

We will follow his example when telling this story. We will describe economic theories as ideas which are supported by scientific evidence, and those which do not have a scientific base we will refer to as mythology, and reject as unfounded. We will deal only with those economic ideas, which we consider central, and of significance to the present situation in the UK, and of relevance to the economy of Scotland.

Through his observations and enquiries into the early development of capitalism, mainly in Glasgow, Smith used his insight to probe into what we would now call economics and came out with some very interesting findings. One of his ideas and the one we will concentrate upon concerned the role of the market in a capitalist exchange system. He showed that the market, although set up primarily by producers of goods and services for their own purposes, soon took on a life of its own, because it brought consumers together and gave them power.

This forced producers to meet the requirements of the consumers rather than those of the producers.

This view of the significance of economics in the 'free market', as an abstract theoretical model, has been at the centre of economic theory ever since and remains so, and virtually all economic theory is related in some degree to this concept - Marxist theory not excluded.

Adam Smith, like every thinker before him, and since, has had his ideas stretched, and distorted well beyond his own conception of them. Today we hear people from the Adam Smith Institute, even here in Scotland, advocating that private capitalism be involved in education in Adam Smith's name; an idea which he himself totally rejected for very sound reasons.

Classical Economics.

After Smith's death he gained great fame as the academic who justified greedy capitalism, and even such greedy capitalists as Margaret Thatcher were keen to praise him, even when they did not properly understand his philosophy.

In this way Adam Smith's 'free market' theory was converted to the 'magic power' of the market, and was developed and exaggerated until it would have been entirely unrecognisable to Smith himself.

A hundred years after his book was published, the 'classical economists' in Britain, who regarded themselves as Adam Smith enthusiasts, were teaching *'laissez-faire'* economics, which postulated that the free market had powers of self regulation and would adjust itself back into 'equilibrium' if left to its own devices and freed from human interference. What Smith had taken pains to show, and prove scientifically, they had turned into an act of faith, or religious belief which requires no evidence or scientific proof. Smith must have turned in his grave at their folly.

We need to look briefly at the ideas put forward by the proponents of 'classical' economics, not because it will enlighten us and show us the way forward, but on the contrary, because this approach failed spectacularly and by doing so showed us clearly what not to do again. We learn more from our previous errors than from our successes, if we just pay attention.

This idea of the all powerful market which lies at the heart of 'classical' economics is a very strong and attractive idea. We know how powerful it is, because, in spite of its gigantic and spectacular world-wide failure, it still remains at the very centre of much economic thinking today. It is indeed one of the myths of our economic history which continues to affect and harm us. It remains a popular idea because it is so simple and easy to understand and apply.

The theory is based on the observable fact put forward by Smith that because a market established by producers gives consumers power and allows them to exercise this power, even at times against the wishes of the producers, so this can then be extended to cover a list of 'extra' powers. It is a convenient assumption, and is only a short step away from attributing additional extraordinary powers to an abstracted market, which becomes entirely divorced from the real people involved.

In this way the impersonal abstract 'market' obtains magical powers which allow it, by itself, to ensure that all elements of production are fully employed, that low prices are established and maintained, and that the highest level of economic efficiency is established.

Now anything which can achieve this in economic terms is very attractive indeed to academics, politicians, business, and people in general. What a great idea! A system which makes the whole complex process of production and distribution in a large and growing economy run at maximum efficiency, and which is self-regulating to keep the economy in this highly desirable condition without the need for Governments, or regulators to do anything. What a great idea! It sounds too good to be true, and of course, back in the real world, it is not true!

The market does not have such magic powers and does not perform like that in the real economy; only in the abstract world of classical economic theory can it exist. We have learned at great cost to real people, that it fails miserably when applied by Governments and businesses in practice, and there are many historical examples of such failures. The great depression of the 1930's was a clear worldwide example, which ended in war and massive human suffering.

So among those of us with a scientific approach to economic matters, what we have learned is that unregulated free markets don't work automatically, and don't necessarily lead to great beneficial outcomes; indeed they often lead to severe hardship. Unfortunately, that lesson has not been learned by everyone. In spite of the clear lessons from history, we are still plagued by people in power who continue to believe the myth about self-regulating markets. The so called neo-liberalism, (or more properly neo-classical), idea is based on this myth, and is once again causing the paralysis of economic potential in the world capitalist system.

Marx and Keynes

Karl Marx *did* understand Smith and his scientific, materialist, approach. He also of course had the views of the 'Classical Economists' to call upon as well. Marx accepted Smith's views on the importance of the market, and the significance of the free market implications for economic theory. Indeed, he founded his economic philosophy on Smith's ideas, but he rejected the 'Classical Economists' mythology about self-regulating markets. He pointed out that far from being 'self-regulating', the market was in fact unstable in two specific ways, and that left to its own devices the market would get out of control.

Even to-day this is still the big and significant division in economic theory. Can a free market manage the economy for us, or do we need to manage the free market?

Marx identified two aspects of the free market which were unstable. It is our view that the main problem we have in the UK today relates to the second of these, but we need to look at his first aspect, because this needs to be understood in relation to our economic history, and indeed the way forward for an independent Scotland.

Today we can observe three distinct examples of economic theory at work;

(1) The Chinese growth model,

(2) The Keynesian model and

(3) The Neo-liberal model.

All of these have their adherents in the international economy, and to the extent that they are successful or otherwise, so their adherents will flourish or decline.

Since we are concerned with the Scottish economy we will leave the Chinese growth model to one side as it is not really appropriate, although it has shown a phenomenal rate of sustained economic growth. If it continues for much longer at the present rate, particularly when capitalist economies are stagnating, then China will soon dominate the world economy and with the other growing BRIC group of countries will be important for Scotland's economic future. However, we will return to more immediate matters.

Marx's first comments on the stability of the market related to the regular fluctuations in the market caused by the exaggerations in investment in capital goods as the result of minor changes in market demand for consumer goods, and how this would lead to regular and increasing market fluctuation if not controlled.

These predictions did of course manifest themselves in ever greater swings in the boom and recession process as he predicted, leading to the appalling depression in 1929 which led to upheaval in the whole capitalist world, fascism, and eventually world war.

The experience however of the market's inherent instability, and its devastating consequences, also led directly to intelligent consideration by many individuals, and by one in particular, John Maynard Keynes, a Cambridge Scholar. Keynes began to look at this problem from 'outside the box' as it were; that is, he put aside all his study of classical economics from Cambridge and looked afresh at all the assumptions around the economic theory of his time. He recognised that the classical theory was badly flawed.

He helped Lloyd-George to write a political leaflet for the Liberals in the 1929 election called *'We can Conquer Unemployment'*. This was the earliest example of his new economic thinking, which later emerged in his now famous book *The General Theory of Employment, Interest and Money,* which was published in 1936.

What Keynes identified was that the market does not have a natural tendency to stable growth in equilibrium, which would ensure that all labour resources are engaged. Indeed the opposite is the case; because of the relative size and significance of capital goods production relative to that of consumer goods. This forces the market out of shape and induces wild fluctuations – often referred to as 'stop-go', or 'boom & bust', or regular recession and recovery.

What Keynes had discovered was in fact a re-discovery of Marx's first way in which the free market was unstable, although Keynes's explanation of the process is much easier to understand than that of Marx. However, Keynes's ideas were ignored by the politicians of the time, and only came to the fore in the Second World War.

To further illustrate the stupidity of classical economic mythology, Britain went into the war in 1939 with a considerable number of unemployed shipbuilders, and for a further year, during the so called 'phony war', we continued to have thousands of unemployed shipyard workers. During that valuable time Germany found work for anyone, they even used imported forced labour to build ships, in an attempt to catch up on Britain's advantage in shipping and with the Royal Navy.

The Second World War demonstrated quite clearly that Keynes was right about 'managing the market', in order to get full productive capacity. Hitler had totally ignored the German classical economists, who advised him that his massive military expenditure and autobahn public expenditure programme would ruin the economy.

To the total surprise of the economists at the time, his programme proved to be good for the economy and the classical economists were entirely wrong and dumbfounded. Keynes had predicted that such a public expenditure programme would work in such circumstances, and was shown to have been right. Churchill recognised that Keynes was ahead of the other economists of his day and appointed him as a senior advisor to his government.

At last, in the official capacity of Chief Economic Advisor to the Churchill government, and then after the war to the Attlee government, Keynes, who was undoubtedly the best economist in the western world at that time, finally had his chance to play an important role in the UK government's economic policy.

In the next chapter we will continue the story by looking at Keynes' ideas as implemented by the Attlee government and copied by many other governments. However before we do that, we need to give some consideration to the development of banking and finance, and the important role this plays in the economic system.

Money is the great mystery of the economic system and is therefore the cause of much confusion and misunderstanding. Paper money, Smith explained, was of great value in trading as a medium of exchange, but it has no intrinsic value. Its value is contained entirely by what it can secure in exchange, nothing more and nothing less. *"If it could be exchanged for nothing"*, he wrote, *"it would, like a bill upon a bankrupt, be of no more value than the most useless piece of paper".*

This is of even greater significance in the UK today than when originally penned all those years ago.

In Adam Smith's time, money in the UK was still backed up by real gold or silver in the bank. When he said that that the *"value"* of money *"was contained entirely by what it can secure in exchange"* he is describing money as an exchange medium, which is its primary purpose in economics. He was not referring to the 'commodity' value of the gold or silver it represented in his day.

Today however we do not have that distinction to concern us. Money in the UK now is not backed by gold or silver. It is what is known as a fiat currency, that is, paper money which is backed up 'by the taxpayer'. We will be dealing with that in much more detail in Part Two, but it might be helpful if we consider some of the economic implications of that now.

If the only value of money is, as Adam Smith says, its exchange value, then this means that there is a close relationship in any market system between the total amount of money and the total amount of goods. If we look at it in very simple terms, and assume a simple model of the UK economy which has no imports or exports, and which is a mere snap-shot in time, then we can see that if the total amount of money in the UK economy was £1 million, then the total amount of goods and services in the UK market would be £1 million. Because, as Smith says, the money has no intrinsic value it merely reflects the exchange value of the goods.

Now suppose the government increased the amount of paper money in circulation by 100% overnight (and again assume that everything else remained the same), then prices would just double, everything would cost twice as much, but since the amount of goods and services remained the same, the total value of the Gross Domestic Product (GDP – the total value of national production) would remain the same in real terms although everything would be dearer.

Taking this relationship a bit further, using the same model, if the total amount of money was increased by 10% each year, and the total amount of goods and services also rose by 10% in the same period, prices would remain static, the GDP would rise by 10% and we would all be 10% better off. Conversely, if the money supply rose by 10% while goods and services remained static then prices would rise by 10% but wealth would remain static.

This will be dealt with in more detail in Part Two, where we discuss the importance of the government keeping control of money supply because clearly if the money supply itself is manipulated and people can make real wealth from such activity then the wealth must come from the production system, not from the money. Manipulating the money or monetary system to extract real wealth from the economy is what we discuss in Part Two and describe as 'Smoke and Mirrors'.

The notion that a hundred pound note is worthless if it cannot be used as a means of exchange, is difficult to accept because of our experience in a market based society. If however, we imagine ourselves shipwrecked on an unpopulated island and having to select a box full of £100 notes or a box of old tools, we would know right away what real values are, because the money would have no exchange value and would therefore be useless, while the old tools would be of great value.

Yet people ask, "If Scotland was independent where would it get the money from to provide a decent health service?" The short answer to that naive question is, Scotland would print the money. The real question should be, would Scotland have the *real resources* in human and material terms to provide a decent health service? Certainly it would, Scotland has all the resources to be among the richest countries per capita in the world.

So this distinction between real wealth and valueless paper money is very important to understand and keep a close eye on. The explanation for the demise of the UK economy can be seen very much more clearly if we strip away the illusion that money is real wealth. It is not, it is merely an exchange token. Most economic problems can be traced back to when these 'tokens' mutated into an abstract commodity to be traded in the free markets, but that is another story for later.

An effective banking system has always been an important key to a developing economy, and it is interesting therefore to consider the early days of banking in Scotland.

After the reformation much former church land had found its way into the hands of the aristocrats, and sheep farming became the centre of the lucrative wool trade. In the towns artisans were turning to small scale manufacturing, and some farmers were keen to try out new forms of agriculture which promised to be more productive.

Now this meant that there were wealthy landowners who had sound assets, mainly land and buildings, but had very little liquidity (wealth which is easy to exchange). This means that the assets they had were tied up in big fixed lumps, such as land and buildings, which are not readily exchangeable for money. The wealthy merchants in the towns also had assets but not land. Thanks to their trading links they had gold and silver, which was easier to convert to money and they therefore had more liquidity.

The artisans and progressive farmers needed small amounts of capital to fund their schemes for investment in their projects, so they were looking for small amounts of capital. Those who needed capital were all individually too small to attract the big landlords who had poor liquidity in any event. The merchants were unlikely to give capital to the artisans, whom they saw as their social inferiors, but they were very keen to try to get hold of land which meant a big step up the social ladder.

The early banks therefore were in a very good position to help all three, and they could do it by merely acting as brokers, circulating the money as a medium of exchange, and charging interest on it. Everyone was a winner. The artisan, progressive farmer, or new capitalist, had access to capital provided he paid a regular payment to the bank. The wealthy landowner had access to cash (liquidity), if he put some land in as security, the merchant got access to interest on his assets and the chance to purchase land when there was a default by any landowner.

The banking system provided an important service to developing capitalism. The Bank of Scotland was established in Edinburgh in 1695. The Royal Bank of Scotland was established also in Edinburgh, in 1727, and the British Linen Company Bank in Glasgow in 1746, although the Linen Bank was initially limited to the burgeoning linen industry in Scotland.

Everything we are discussing here was very small in relation to our current view of Scotland. In terms of population it is estimated that in 1755 there was a total of 1,265,000 living in Scotland, half of them in the Highlands.

Population was growing fast, and shifting from the Highlands to the south, so that by 1821 there were 2,091,000 people in Scotland, with around 60% of them in the south.

These banks were small and catered for an equally small section of the population, located mainly in Edinburgh and Glasgow, with agents in the other towns. In 1755, Edinburgh was by far the largest town in Scotland with a population of 57,000, while Glasgow's population at that time was 31,700. It was not until 1821 that Glasgow had a larger population than Edinburgh, with 147,000, compared to Edinburgh's 138,000.

In the early days everything was on a much smaller scale. It has been estimated that the total assets of Scottish banks were only £600,000 in 1750, but had risen to £3,700,000 by 1770, which was just 5 years before Adam Smith's famous book was published.

Bankers had discovered that if you kept 10% of your liquid assets in reserve in order to meet depositor's normal requirements, you could use the other 90% to lend out and charge interest. This system worked reasonably well for many years because the operation was relatively small, and because the bank assets were based on gold and silver coinage which was acceptable, and exchangeable, across the trading world at that time.

Over time there were of course problems in the banking industry which needed adjustment, the main one being the acceptance and development of joint-stock banking in Scotland, which was copied from Holland. This provided a more flexible model than the old family dominated banking system.

Before we leave this period of great historical change and development however, within which the Scottish banking system spent its early adolescence, it might be of interest to note the changes in people's occupation, as recorded between Edinburgh (more traditional), and Glasgow (new developments).

Occupation:	Edinburgh 1773	Glasgow 1783
Nobles and Gentry	5.2%	1%
Professional Men	28.8%	12.3%
Merchants & Manufacturers	12.5%	30%
Artisans, Craftsmen & Small Traders	30.5%	42.1%*

The employment titles are of course old style, but the important thing is the changing trend. This gives a flavour of the changes taking place in the period when Adam Smith was observing developments in Glasgow.

CHAPTER 2

Keynes and the Unstable Market

John Maynard Keynes

In telling the story of the economic journey in Britain's history, there must be a clear distinction between economic theory and mythology. This is important if we are to understand the lessons of our own history. There is an old saying familiar to most of us, but studiously ignored by politicians and classical economists, *"Those who fail to learn the lessons of the past are doomed to repeat them."*

Economic theory is an idea, or set of ideas, which can be tested like any other scientific theory, and which becomes acceptable and applicable only when it has passed the test.

'Economic mythology' is an idea, or set of ideas, which are not designed for testing, and which we are required to accept by 'faith' alone, not by evidence or scientific testing.

We live in a scientific age, unlike our ancestors, and therefore we know that any theory, however interesting, should be tested to see if it can perform as predicted before we put too much reliance on it. So how do we test economic theory?

The only way we can effectively test theories about macro economics is to try them out on the real economy at macro (whole economy) level. That is, we need the authority of the government to implement policies at particular times, and in circumstances which effect the whole economy, and then to observe how the economy will perform. Obviously it is not often that an academic economist gets that opportunity. John Maynard Keynes was however the exception.

As touched upon earlier, Keynes had helped write a political leaflet for the Liberals in 1929 called, *'We can conquer unemployment'*, so the idea of full employment was very much at

the heart of his economic philosophy. However his theories needed testing in the real world, and initially that did not seem likely at all.

Keynes's involvement in the 1929 General Election therefore was with the Liberals. Labour won 287 seats in the General Election, with the Tories in second place gaining 261 seats, so again, as in 1924, Labour formed a coalition Government with the Liberals. The Labour leadership with Ramsay MacDonald as Prime Minister, and Philip Snowden as Chancellor, were still very much under the influence of the Classical Economists, Alfred Marshall and Arthur Pigou, who had been Keynes' tutors at Cambridge. Indeed, the Tories, and even most of the Liberals, were still very much trapped in the classical mythology about economic matters while incomes fell and unemployment rose.

In 1931 Keynes was Chairman of the Government's Economic Advisory Committee and published a report suggesting more public investment in order to tackle unemployment. This was instantly attacked as being outwith the economic beliefs of the day, and the Labour Chancellor, Philip Snowden, laughed at it and called it 'economic nonsense'.

So Keynes's views were ignored, and the coalition government stumbled on to further economic disaster which they tried desperately to put right by making cuts in public expenditure and applying means-testing for welfare benefits.

Is it not strange how his ignorance and arrogance seems so familiar to us to-day?

We know from history that the failure of the Labour led coalition government to even consider Keynes's advice was an economic and political catastrophe. If Britain, with a Labour led government, had started the world economic recovery in 1931, could they have influenced the events which followed in Germany in 1933, and which led directly to world war? Who knows?

However we should have learned to be careful when the people are being told by their political leaders that the economic system is broken, and the politicians can't mend it without long and difficult sacrifices by the people. We know that this situation led to Fascism in the 1930's and we are seeing Fascism rising up again in peoples' despair. When will we ever learn?

During the war the government was forced to 'think outside the box', and to consider how objectives could be gained by any means possible, or even by some which looked impossible.

In this situation Churchill recognised that Keynes had understood the economic situation much better than most economists, and he installed him into an important position in the coalition, with the result that when the Attlee government was elected in 1945, Keynes was there to advise the cabinet how to run the post-war economy.

The Attlee Government 1945-51.

The first Labour majority government under Clement Attlee was by any measure the most successful the UK has ever experienced, judged by the benefits which it provided to the British people. It was a remarkably successful administration which delivered a phenomenal range of achievements. Moreover, it did so over a very short time, and in the most difficult of circumstances.

It was the achievements of this government which gave the Labour Party such a great reputation among working people in Britain and particularly in Scotland. To this day it still constitutes the core of Labour Party support, even if the present New Labour Party leadership pay little respect to this history. Indeed, they are actively trying to disown it. So we need to look at the achievements of the Attlee government and the role played by Keynes in advising it.

One point virtually ignored by UK history is the leadership style of Attlee himself. Unlike Churchill or Thatcher, he did not get a State funeral, or get his statue in Westminster, but he was a far more effective leader in a democracy than either of them. He acted as a co-ordinator of his powerful and diverse cabinet and once cabinet decisions were made, he acted decisively to ensure that they were implemented. In a democratic organisation that is how

23

leaders should operate, only a monarchy, or fascist organisation, needs a strong all powerful leader. A democratic society works better with a co-ordinator.

Clement Attlee was a London lawyer who served in the army, he was promoted to major because he was considered good at co-ordinating others and directing team efforts, and that undoubtedly was his skill. When Churchill made him Deputy Prime Minister in 1942 in the war-time coalition government, he said, *"Attlee was a modest man, with much to be modest about"*. Well Attlee certainly was not a braggart.

Although the war in Europe was over before the 1945 General Election, the war in the East was still going on. The election saw the Labour Party win a landslide victory. They secured 48% of the vote, and gained 393 seats, while Churchill's Tories managed a mere 213 seats. This was one of the rare occasions when the Scottish voters got the government they voted for, as did the Welsh voters. Labour was able to form its first majority government, with a number of experienced ministers from the war-time coalition government and the foremost economist in the western world as their chief economic advisor. The stage was set for something different.

However, the task faced by the Attlee government was awesome. Britain was flat broke, with a huge national debt to pay for war materials we had been getting from the USA and others. A large number of working men in their prime years were in uniform, many of them abroad, and many in prisoner-of-war camps. Many more were dead, leaving families without a breadwinner. Our industrial base had been flogged to exhaustion to produce war equipment and supplies which were now surplus to requirements, factories needed major investment in order to change to peace-time production. These factors alone would have been enough to be dealing with, there was however a great deal more.

Our trading partners in Europe were devastated, and were in no condition for effective trading. Britain's colonial empire was in open revolt, and was demanding freedom.

Wide divisions were appearing between our recent American and Russian allies, creating new world tensions.

In the middle of this chaotic situation, the Attlee government set about its task to:

- Create a National Health Service

- Nationalise, and invest heavily in the mining industry

- Nationalise and invest in energy supply and distribution

- Nationalise and invest in the steel industry

- Nationalise the railways and public transport system

- Vastly improve education all over the UK

- Initiate massive public and private house-building

- Establish the basis of the welfare system

- Nationalise the Bank of England

It would take a lot of imagination to visualise any government today even contemplating such a workload, let alone initiating and managing it.

These are only the major parts of its manifesto which were achieved. It did a lot more in terms of public health, and a wide range of other developments, and significantly, it maintained full employment. At the end of this short period of majority Labour government, the British working people did get a considerable shift in the distribution of National Income (GDP or Gross Domestic Product), in their favour, particularly by the use of the 'social wage' through universal benefits. It is sad to reflect that the Labour leadership today, who are political pygmies compared with the labour political giants of 1945, want to dismantle universal benefits.

This government also played a leading role in the Nuremberg Trials and the establishment of the World Court, together with the establishment of the United Nations, and it started on the road to dismantle the old colonial system by negotiating political freedom for India, Pakistan, Ceylon, Burma and Jordan.

So how did the Attlee government pay for the NHS? Where did they find the money to buy the mining industry, the railways, the steelworks etc., and then to invest heavily in all of them? How could they afford to spend money on education, public health, and on agriculture, in spite of the country being flat broke, and already in record debt? How was it done?

They took Keynes' advice, and followed a Keynesian policy. This is how it works.

You will recall that Keynes was very focused on curing unemployment. His approach was simple in essence, although perhaps difficult for classical economists to understand.

He starts by rejecting the 'myth' that the free market is self-regulating, and that left to itself the market will bring into employment all available labour and natural resources.

He said that if the government wanted the market to work effectively they must get involved in managing it. Where there are large unemployed pools of labour, then the government must invest resources into the areas it wants to stimulate, and employ those resources. This in turn will create 'new' wealth which can be reinvested by what he called 'the multiplier effect', which will in turn create more new wealth.

There is no magic involved, it is all quite simple and scientific, and it is easy to understand where the 'new' wealth comes from. If all wealth comes from putting labour and materials together in a work environment, as indeed it does, then it follows that if you have unemployed labour and materials (natural resources), then, if the government ensures that they are put together under effective working conditions, then they will both increase national income (GDP) i.e. make more products, and at the same time reduce public expenditure (reduce unemployment benefit). That is clearly a winning and effective combination.

That is the essence of a Keynesian policy. It is of course more sophisticated to deal with the type of investment, the monetary and fiscal policy, and the nature of the multiplier, particularly in an open trading economy, but this is the heart of the theory and why it works.

It is important for us today to be aware of the basic elements of Keynes's economic theory because people frequently claim to be Keynesian in their economic ideas when they are clearly not. Keynes's name is used to cover for quite different and quite incompatible economic policies.

By way of example, in early 2013, Alastair Darling MP, the last Labour Chancellor of the Exchequer, claimed in a full page article in the *Scotland on Sunday* newspaper that he was, 'an unashamed Keynesian'. In a reader's letter reacting to the article, he was invited to explain why anyone should associate any kind of shame with Keynesian economics. He was also asked a number of questions about his actions in handing over taxpayer's money to the banks, and about his reported claim that the Westminster government would need to make greater cuts in public spending than Thatcher had made. Alastair did not respond.

Having started the debate on Keynesianism in the press, he clearly felt unable to defend his claims.

We might draw Alastair's attention to Joseph Stiglitz's book, '*Freefall*', (*Free Markets and the sinking of the Global Economy*), where this Noble Peace Prize (Economics 2001) winning economist is highly critical of what the Governments who bailed out the super banks did. Stiglitz writes, "*Spending money to bail out banks without getting something in return, gives money to the richest and has almost no multiplier effec*t".

So here Joseph Stiglitz is making his view clear, that bailing out the banks was anti-Keynesian because it put potential government investment into the wrong hands, and produced no Keynesian multiplier effect.

If you compare the Keynesian approach to that of the neo-liberal, who has no answer to rising youth unemployment, it becomes crystal clear which of them is the sensible, scientific approach. The neo-liberal would not dispute that putting labour and other resources together will create wealth and would acknowledge that this was so. However the free market disciple would insist that the government should not interfere, and should stand back and allow the markets to find their own way back to full employment.

The truth is the market cannot do this by itself. Indeed if you reduce public expenditure you will create a multiplier in the opposite direction, which drives employment and income in the other direction downward, unless there is heavy investment in the private sector.

However, if demand in the economy is falling, private investment is less likely to be attracted. That is why this approach has consistently failed, as it is doing again now. You could not pay your household debts by reducing your working hours, neither can the national economy.

So we will return to the physical evidence again. Keynes advised the Attlee government to take firm control of the Bank of England and monetary policy. He advised them to find employment for the thousands of military conscripts who were leaving the forces, by means of public investment into the important industries required for a manufacturing economy, and to use nationalisation (which was the Labour Party policy), as the vehicle for this directed investment.

This meant that every person who left the military and went into employment added new wealth to the national income and reduced public expenditure in the same way as converting unemployed to employed people will do. This meant that, although national expenditure was rising steadily during the years of the Attlee government, national income was rising faster and therefore was able to sustain the investment.

That is in essence how it worked. The government was increasing public debt for investment, but this led to increasing national real income for most people and also increasing government tax income to pay back the debt. It was what is called a '**virtuous circle**' in economics, where everyone benefits and there are no losers. In contrast, when government cuts public investment, which reduces demand through the 'multiplier', which causes more unemployment, which reduces demand further etc., that is called a '**vicious circle**' where everyone is a loser. You might recognise the latter as the present UK Government's way of trying to tackle the present economic difficulty.

Keynes's advice enabled the Attlee government to climb steadily out of a deep economic hole. If that policy was so effective in acquiring state assets for the country, maintaining full employment, raising incomes and eroding inequality - why then did we stop applying such a clearly effective formula?

You will appreciate that the growth in 'new wealth' which this policy can create is only possible when there is a pool of unemployed workers, or, as in this case, of people being discharged from the military. It also applies where there is high immigration, in other words any situation where there is a pool of new labour which can be drawn into production.

Once the economy approaches near full employment the Keynesian policy moves on to maintaining that equilibrium. The objective then is not for the government to invest to stimulate additional labour into production, but to manage the economy to maintain full employment and encourage movement towards increasing productivity.

It is a lot easier to apply Keynesian policies to achieve the first objective; than it is to achieve the second.

However the experience of the Attlee government was noted elsewhere in Europe, and was copied in many other countries, particularly in Scandinavia. Where this is the case you will observe five characteristics about such countries.

1. They have more government control and regulation of the economy
2. They are far more egalitarian
3. They have a high social wage and have well developed trade-union organisation
4. They are among the wealthiest (per capita) countries in the world
5. They have relatively low unemployment.

This should be our aspiration for the new Scotland. We do not need to look to Scandinavia for our inspiration, we can find it in our own history and build on it from there, but there are obstacles in our way.

In the following chapters we shall look at some of these and how to deal with them.

CHAPTER 3

Keynsian Economic Development Internationally

Keynesian Development

The Attlee government had been so successful economically, that its Keynesian economic policies were being copied elsewhere in the world.

This resulted in Keynesian economics being seen everywhere in the western world as being the new economics of capitalism. The' classical' economics which had been dominant for so long in capitalist countries were demoted and regarded as out-dated and old hat. There was however still one area of exception to this, the USA.

In its attempt to regenerate the European economy after the devastation of the Second World War, the USA played a significant role as the economic powerhouse which would give muscle to the efforts. Keynes however, was undoubtedly the brains behind it.

In July 1944, at Bretton Woods in New Hampshire, a significant event took place. It was called the United Nations Monetary & Finance Conference which was held in advance of the setting up of the United Nations, which was itself established the following year.

This Bretton Woods conference, as it became known, looked towards the end of the war in Europe and post-war arrangements for monetary and economic development in that area.

The conference was attended by J.M. Keynes as a representative of the British (War-Time) Coalition Government. The IMF (International Monetary Fund) was established at this conference, and much consideration was given to post-war reconstruction in Europe.

This early work in America was developed much further again, with Keynes' involvement on behalf of the Attlee government, towards the American Marshall plan which was announced later in 1947, after Keynes himself had died. Thus was Keynesian policy adapted to European redevelopment.

The USA would play the role of the 'Government' and would get involved in heavy investment in certain industries, in particular countries geared towards sustained growth of the national economies of these different countries, and to the redevelopment of the European economy.

This of course was in stark contrast to what had happened after the First World War. It was from this development that the European Coal & Steel Treaty developed, which was signed in Paris in 1951, and it is from this that the present European Union has its origins.

So the Attlee government firmly tested the Keynesian theory and established it as valid, and science based. Moreover, it had helped to spread its development, particularly in Europe and throughout the commonwealth.

However, in Britain there was a backlash. The Tories had never accepted the Keynesian revolution and they fought tooth and nail against it. It is often forgotten now that the Tories were vigorously opposed to the NHS and that the BMA, undoubtedly with encouragement from the Tories, organised a doctors' strike - or boycott, of the NHS.

Aneurin Bevan was the brilliant young Minister and son of a Welsh miner who had put the Health Service Bill through the Commons. He needed all the fighting spirit and tenacity he could muster to overcome the fierce Conservative opposition.

Keynesianism Undermined

The Tories, and their friends in big business and the media, were bitterly opposed to the whole economic thrust of the Attlee government, and they united with some backsliders from the Labour ranks to undermine the popular Labour government's economic policy. Their media supporters ran a relentless campaign against the Labour government, blaming them for every conceivable problem, and in particular, they attacked them for continuing to ration essential commodities.

Rationing had, of course, arisen from war-time shortages, but many on the left found rationing helpful to those on low incomes because shops could not push up prices on food and clothing and other vital goods to put them beyond the range of the poor. However the Labour government's own economic success meant that people were getting wealthier, and now they too began to feel that rationing was restricting them.

After a relentless barrage of media propaganda aimed at the Labour government, and significant changes in constituency boundaries, the Tories finally won power in the UK parliament after two general elections. In the election of February 1950, Labour won 315 seats to the Tories 295 with the Liberals on 9, so Labour retained an overall majority. However, there was a strong right-wing cabal in the Labour Party causing internal division around issues, such as putting a charge on NHS prescriptions which had been free. This internal bickering in the Labour Party undermined the Labour government, making them unable to govern effectively, and they were forced to go back to the electorate in October the following year.

In the 1951 election, the Tories with their associates (mainly in Northern Ireland), won a 16 seat majority, with a total of 321 seats to Labour's 295 and the Liberals 6. The media, with right-wing Labour support, had finally been successful in getting the Tories into power in Westminster, but did they win over the people? Well, that is debatable, because the Tories and their associates got 51.36% of the seats in the Westminster Parliament with 39.29% of the votes cast. So the majority of the voters rejected the Tories. It was the undemocratic Westminster voting system that gave power to the Tories. They did not win it. You need to study the voting figures to expose the anomaly.

However, the Tories knew that their hold on power was very tenuous. In spite of their strong opposition to much that the Labour government had done, they were in no position to change it. So they accepted the NHS, they accepted the nationalized coal mines, power generation and distribution. They accepted the nationalized railways and buses. They accepted the welfare system; but most importantly, they accepted Keynesian full-employment economic policy and were obliged to maintain it.

Keynes himself had died in 1946, but his economic theory long outlived him. Even the return to power of the Tories in the UK could not kill off the economic legacy which he had left. It took another 25 years before the UK government would directly challenge Keynesian economics, and finally displace his influence in the UK and across much of Europe.

Having achieved near full employment, Keynesian policies were less clear on how to manage markets towards maintaining this. Making advances in productivity, limiting inflation, and maintaining a healthy balance of payments, is a much more sophisticated application of economic management, particularly when unemployment is low, for any government to apply.

If there is no pool of unemployed labour to draw upon, then government investment in the economy can lead to overheating. Similarly, the printing of new money which cannot bring unemployed resources into production, because there are none, will merely cause price inflation.

From the chart on Page 35 it can be seen that while unemployment under the Attlee government had fallen to 3% by 1951, the maintenance of full employment continued to be a problem for all governments in the UK until around 1969 when Keynesian policies began to be rejected. The chart shows what then happened.

There is however a distinct possibility that Keynesian type policies could be reintroduced in an independent Scotland and this is specifically catered for in Part Two.

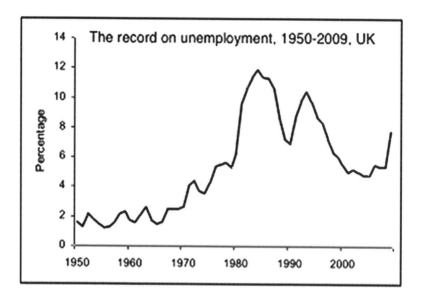

Neo-Liberalism

There was an entirely different attitude to these matters in the USA as Keynesianism had never been embraced by American economists. It simply did not seem relevant in post-war America. Over and above a buoyant domestic demand, this was compounded by the application of Keynesian economic policies in the UK and Europe, which had vastly increased incomes and trade in Europe. As the main investor in this, the USA benefited significantly from this trade and made a fortune. Its factories were extremely busy meeting the demand thus created. America was the land of opportunity and full employment. It did not need Keynes, or so it seemed. The truth was of course, that America was growing in wealth *because* of Keynesian policies in the UK and Europe, not in spite of them.

In 1946 when Keynes's ideas were beginning to show results, a 34 year old American economics professor, Milton Friedman, who rejected Keynes' economic ideas and particularly his challenge to the free market mythology, took up a new post at Chicago

University faculty of Economics. He went on to found the Chicago School of Economics, which was later to be at the centre of the campaign against the dominance of Keynes in the post-war period.

Others, such as Friedrich Hayek, who was born in Austria, but came to Britain to escape the Nazis and took British nationality, also challenged Keynesian economics from a free market position. Hayek was 56 in 1946. These two men, and their 'Chicago School' and 'Austrian School' colleagues, were the founders of what became 'Neo-Liberalism', the new challenge to Keynesianism in the 1970's.

Both these men learned their economics, like Keynes, in the so called classical period. They had been taught to believe that the free market was self-regulating. Indeed it was Keynes' rejection of this same dogma or untested myth, which the neo-liberals reacted to. Since Keynes' challenge had been by practical example, which the Attlee Government had implemented and in so doing provided the physical proof of Keynesian economic theory, the Neo-Liberalist economists had to present their untested mythology against Keynes' tested theory, which was not an easy thing to do. They did however have substantial financial backing. Given past and current experience, it is for the reader to judge if Neo-Liberalism has provided any vestige of proof that their theory is anything more than myth.

Neo-Liberalism relies on the belief, or blind faith, one might have in the assertion that the free market is self-regulating. No evidence of that assertion is offered. They merely suggest how the economy *might* respond in certain given circumstances (*if this myth is correct*).

Neo-Liberalism is not, and never has been, an intellectual debate. It is a reaction to Keynesianism much like the initial reaction to Darwinism. It is shock and disgust that someone should challenge a sacred belief that carries so many hopes and dreams and that has been around so long. It was not however Keynes's ideas that undermined capitalism, any more than it was Darwin's ideas which undermined religion. If you base your economic ideas, on maintaining a myth which scientific examination and testing shows to be unsustainable, then who do you blame if it fails?

There were real economic problems in Britain in the 1960's and 70's. Britain was constantly losing out in the growth of world trade, and as a country very much dependent on manufacturing, this was a big problem. There was no simple explanation or cure at that time.

The heart of the problem was that those countries which had been devastated during the war had built their factories or engineering plants anew, and had equipped them with the latest technologies. Britain on the other hand remained stuck with old and out-dated factories and plants. This meant that productivity in these UK industries was not able to compete with the more modern plants. Thus productivity as a whole in the UK was falling behind, and needed to be addressed.

One can seldom explain something as complex as the UK economy by reference to a single factor. In economics one factor normally relates to another because it is a dynamic system. However, with that clear understanding, we would suggest that the fundamental problem for the UK economy at that time, was that it had gone through a period of sustained low level of investment in manufacturing industry. Higher investment in that area would have enabled the manufacturing base to remain competitive. In a quickly developing world market, all the UK needed to do for growth in exports, was to maintain its level of 'relative' productivity, but it failed significantly in this respect.

In a modern economy, it makes no sense to say that your workers failed to keep up with some other country's workers because they were lazy, or took too many tea breaks, or whatever. The main factor in securing high productivity is investment. If your workers are trying to plough a field with two horses, while the German workers are using a ten drill tractor then they will do it better, faster, and more accurately, irrespective of how many tea breaks they take. The average German worker is not significantly different or better than the average Scot, or English, or French worker, but if they are all doing the same job, and one of them has better equipment to do that job, then he/she will do it better.

That is why good modern factories, with the latest equipment, (investment), enjoy high productivity, or the ability for each worker to produce more in the same time period. That was the problem in the UK, but that is not what was disseminated by the politicians and media.

If you look at the British media during that period you will find endless stories about lazy British workers, or wages being too high in Britain, or trade-unions which have too much power, all causing economic problems for Britain. If you look at political party policies in that period you find 'incomes policies', 'trade-union restriction policies', 'price and income policies' etc. These are the symptoms of the neo-liberal agenda which has presided over the steady economic decline of the United Kingdom these past fifty years.

In the meantime, in the economics faculties of British Universities, there was a full scale assault on Keynesian ideas. The neo-liberal attack was under way in the academic world to undermine Keynesianism. It was not a head-on challenge, if it had been, there is no doubt that Keynesian economics would have won easily; it was much more subtle than that. It sowed seeds of doubt which challenged the long term effects of Keynesianism - on inflation, on productivity and on monetary policy.

While students and tutors in economics could be confident that Keynes' theories had been clearly proven and established in the context of dealing with major unemployment, the same could not be said for its performance in times of full employment. The neo-liberals latched on to this and focused upon this as a 'weakness' in the theory. The fact that this weakness was no more or less significant than any other unproven theory was conveniently set aside. Thus Keynes was dismissed to make room for the more doctrinaire mantra of neo-liberalism.

By the mid-seventies the various forms of neo-liberalism were obviously penetrating the civil service, because government ministers started to make anti-Keynesian pronouncements, which usually means that the lobbyists were hard at work in the corridors of Westminster.

An interesting example of this is from a speech by James Callaghan to the Labour Party Conference in 1976. Sunny Jim, the close friend of the trade-unions, told the conference, "We used to think that we could spend our way out of a recession and increase employment – by boosting government spending. I tell you in all candour that that option no longer exists." He went on, "We must ask ourselves unflinchingly, what is the cause of high unemployment? Quite simply and unequivocally, it is caused by paying ourselves more than the value of what we produce."

That is a clear rejection of Keynesian economics by a Labour Chancellor of the Exchequer a whole three years before Margaret Thatcher came into power. It is often said that Thatcher introduced neo-liberalism, but that is not true. The struggle against Keynesianism had been active and strongly founded and supported since 1946 at least, and involved the Tory party, the media and a host of academics and civil servants - indeed the bulk of the British Establishment. It took some considerable time before it started to influence governments and win public acquiescence. Only then could Margaret Thatcher force it through.

This ideology won political power when, in defiance of a TUC policy for investment and development, the Callaghan government resisted the demand of low paid workers in the so called dirty jobs strike in the 'winter of discontent' in 1978-9. This provided Margaret Thatcher with her election slogan that, 'Labour isn't working', and an election victory in 1979.

Of course Thatcher made no bones about it, she was going to take on the Unions, and get the economy going with the 'new' economic ideas promoted by her political guru, Sir Keith Joseph, a disciple of Milton Friedman and his free market philosophy. At last neo-liberalism had broken cover and was to become official Government policy.

However the announcement of neo-liberalism and its early implementation did not mean that it was in a secure position in Britain. It only became so because of two entirely unrelated factors which just happened to turn up at the right moment for Mrs Thatcher.

Thatcher's suppression of public investment was starting to have its initial effect, through the multiplier of creating mass unemployment - in 3 years she had over 3 million unemployed in the UK.

This was causing great restriction on demand and was heading towards deeper recession, which would have caused a balance of payments problem and probably a run on sterling in the international money markets. Then almost out of the blue, North Sea oil started to come ashore in substantial quantities in Aberdeen. This put tax revenue into the UK governments account, it gave a boost to the private sector for investment, and it altered significantly the balance of payments all in one go.

And so North Sea oil coming on stream at precisely the right moment saved the Thatcher Government from severe economic embarrassment.

With unemployment running at over 3 million however, which had not happened in the UK since before the war in pre-Keynesian days, people in Britain were very angry. They held the Thatcher government responsible for this economic disaster. Opinion polls all recorded Margaret Thatcher as having the lowest rating for any Prime Minister since polling began.

She was facing a general election with massive unemployment, economic recession, and appalling opinion poll ratings.

Then she had her second stroke of luck - Argentina invaded the Falkland Islands. She was in her element. Adopting her natural aggressive stance, she assured Britain and the world that the British army would get down there without delay, and recover the Islands. Not without some considerable logistical difficulty and a bit of luck, a well trained professional army was pitched against a mainly conscript opposition. The British forces did the business and returned home as conquering heroes.

The Falklands victory produced a magical transformation of Margaret Thatcher's political appeal in England. This surge of the old colonialism, which gloried in the success of the British army in defending one of the UK's few remaining colonies, did seem to divide political opinion between the people in Scotland and those in England, but in any event, it certainly saved The Iron Lady.

At the election in June 1983 Mrs Thatcher won a resounding 144 seat majority. Even so, once again the election results, if considered just by the actual number of seats gained, does not reflect the full story. The Tories lost 700,000 votes in this election compared to 1979, yet still secured 61.08% of the seats having won only 30.84% of the votes. Of course this was strongly influenced by the right-wing desertion from the Labour Party, which formed the SDP, and which went into the election as the SDP/Liberal Alliance.

The 1983 General Election was in a sense the first time that neo-liberalism was presented to the British public as an option, because by that time it was clear that the main distinction between Keynesian economics and neo-liberalism was an economy run and managed on a full-employment basis, as opposed to one having no Government intervention in an economy with the 'free market' able to take its own unfettered course.

Contrary to 'popular history', provided by the media in the UK which claims that Thatcher and her neo-liberalism were popular with the people, the electoral evidence proves otherwise. Thatcher and neo-liberalism was rejected by 69.16% of the UK electorate at that election. It was however clear that almost institutionalised unemployment, was to be the price that had to be paid for virtually unregulated free markets.

That chimed with that labour party conference in 1976 when Callaghan famously stated that unemployment was caused by high wages and nothing else. He further suggested that if wages in the UK were reduced then we could expect the economy and employment to thrive. That somewhat childlike economic theory has now been entirely disproved by testing in the real economy. Events over recent decades have exposed it as not only anti-Keynesian rhetoric, but entirely baseless.

Callaghan, Thatcher, and the other neo-liberal politicians who followed them, of both the New Labour and Tory variety, succeeded in reducing wages as a percentage of GDP, therefore leaving a greater share for capital. Wages in 1975 amounted to 70.6% of Gross Domestic Product (GDP) (national income), while in 2010 wages represented only 62.6% of GDP in Britain. Quite clearly, much less of the total much larger national income was going into wages and salaries, and much more was going to capital. That part of the strategy was achieved as wages were reduced as a percentage of total income, just as Callaghan said they should. Unfortunately for neo-liberal theory the rest of the strategy was a failure. Unemployment was not wiped out and has remained consistently higher. Indeed, it is now more than double what it was in his day.

In Chapter Five we apply this hard historical evidence to the traditional theoretical model of the elements of production which significantly increases the accuracy of the predictions.

CHAPTER 4

Thatcherism and New Labour

Much has been heard about Thatcherism and how she changed Britain, so what exactly is Thatcherism? She certainly sorted out the militant unions. When I first went to work in Blairhall colliery in Fife in 1953, there were over 100 coal mines in Scotland, and thousands of miners in the National Union of Mineworkers (NUM). The NUM was militant in representing their member's interests. Maggie sorted them out.

There are no militant NUM members in Scotland now. Indeed there are no miners, and no mines left. There are however great scars in the landscape in some parts of Scotland, where coal has been dug up on open-cast operations, but these are now in financial trouble, and the mess has now been left for the public to clear up while our coal now comes from Poland.

This is typical of the Thatcher approach to the economy. Smash the unions or 'the enemy within', as she called them, even if you have to smash the industry at the same time. Talk about throwing the baby out with the bath water. So many of the trade-union militants have now gone, unfortunately, as has most of the heavy industry and manufacturing sector where they used to work.

Britain's economic future could only be viable if it remained a manufacturing country able to sell its products in a competitive world market. The glory days of Empire are dead and gone, and fortunately will never return. If the UK has a role in the modern world, it is as an efficient manufacturer, a role in which we have some considerable experience.

The real problem we had in the 1960's and 70's was not addressed by Thatcher at all in the 1980's, nor has it featured in any government policy since.

The UK has a chronic need for substantial investment in plant and equipment if it is to develop a sound manufacturing base. By and large this has been ignored, with a handful of exceptions, prominent among these being Rolls-Royce, but these exceptions serve only to prove the rule. Even Rolls-Royce went bankrupt in 1971, and was only saved because it was nationalized by the Heath Tory government at that time.

This failure to address solid fundamental aspects of the economy and the eternal search for a quick return, the quick buck, seems to be the Thatcher legacy to the UK, and it is a medicine which is slowly killing the patient.

The Thatcher legacy will be remembered as the de-industrialisation of the UK and the ascendancy of financial engineering. It remains to be seen whether or not the UK can survive and flourish in the 21st century without a manufacturing base. The signs are not promising. If, as David Cameron claims, "We are all Thatcherites now", then that can only mean that politicians from all the main political parties at Westminster accept that a manufacturing base is no longer of significance.

By 1997, manufacturing, which was still falling in importance within the UK economy, remained at 20% of the UK GDP, employing 4.5 million people, while financial services represented 6.5% of GDP.

By 2007 however, manufacturing had fallen to a mere 12.5% of GDP with only 3 million employees, while financial services were now 8.5% of GDP. None of the politicians from any of the Westminster parties seem concerned about that, yet this is undermining the UK economy, and putting all its eggs in one basket, and, as we saw in 2008, a pretty dodgy basket.

Why did Mrs Thatcher move the economy in that direction? What was her objective and motivation? It is difficult to find a rational economic explanation for her behaviour, but why should we expect anything else?

Margaret Thatcher never understood economics and was very selective in her choice of economic ideas. She adopted those sound bites which fitted her political beliefs no matter how incompatible they might be. In this respect she was little different from so many politicians who feel the need to justify their views with economic quotes – no matter how irrelevant or abstruse.

There is a view that Margaret Thatcher drifted into an economic situation rather than by choice. She was very much a product of 'class warfare', in that she had been on the edge of working class, or lower middle class if you prefer, as the daughter of a shop keeper. The family struggled to send her to university for an education, and a step up the class ladder. So Margaret was very class conscious and knew what she was against, rather than what she was for.

No doubt she had also observed that the post-war Labour government had been very successful in re-distributing income towards the working class. In her new class environment, she would have recognised how unpopular this was within the Tory establishment, and with whom she had cast her political lot.

By the time Margaret became leader of the opposition confronting James Callaghan across the dispatch box, she was no doubt well aware that the British establishment were anti-Keynesian. This included much of the Labour leadership, as we have seen and so there was little opposition to her adoption of an openly neo-liberal programme entirely appropriate for an ambitious Tory leader.

The Big Bang.

The Big Bang may turn out to be Thatcher's most enduring contribution to capitalism. It was an event which received very little attention at the time because only a handful of people understood the implications.

In October 1986, Thatcher and her close associate Ronald Reagan performed a ceremony in London to announce '*Big Bang*'. As she explained to a largely bemused electorate, this would free up the London banks and financial services industry from the 'excessive' regulation and control which was preventing these private companies from reaching their full potential.

Having done away with banking regulation in the UK Ronald Reagan carried the torch of reform back to the USA and introduced similar changes which eventually led to the repeal of the Glass-Steagall Act in 2000. This 'freeing up' of the banks from regulation, opened a Pandora's Box. The consequences of which are more properly dealt with in Part Two.

Margaret Thatcher did not do any of this by design; she did it by prejudice, ignorance and a domineering personality. She never intended to bankrupt Britain any more than she intended to make Tories unelectable in Scotland. She managed to do both, just by following her instincts.

New Labour.

Tony Blair and Gordon Brown were the architects of New Labour. The first act of the Blair/Brown partnership in government was to free the Bank of England from government direction and to confirm that they would stick to the previous Tory government's financial policies. This was a signal to the financial sector that New Labour were fully signed up to light touch banking regulation, and to the banks, that they were not going to pursue Keynesian policies to reduce unemployment, all very much in the Thatcher image.

The New Labour governments which followed on from 1997 until 2010 were neo-liberal in their economic policies and they blindly followed the Thatcher route. As a result manufacturing became even weaker, and the banks and financial sector grew stronger. The market was king, and unemployment remained high. The government was neutral when confronted by naked market power. A new class of the excluded poor now began to grow up together with an explosive development of the elite of super-rich in the UK.

In spite of much talk from the New Labour leadership about helping low-income families, and some measures introduced to assist in this, the fact is that inequality increased to the extent that the UK became the fourth most unequal society in the world.

The one lasting and significant contribution of New Labour was to honour its commitment to a Scottish Devolution Bill, and this time the votes of a simple majority would be honoured. New Labour was committed to this because the pressure for an effective devolution bill had enjoyed popular support throughout Scotland. That pressure came not only from the political parties, but also from the trade-unions and churches, and a host of social organisations.

The late Labour Party leader, John Smith, had been personally deeply committed to devolution, and in preparing for the election this had formed a central plank of their Scottish appeal.

John Smith died before the election and this meant a change in the leadership, but the commitment to Scottish devolution was firmly established by then. There is suspicion that had it been possible, Blair would have tried to drop this commitment, he did in fact accept Michael Forsyth's idea that there should be a double vote at the referendum, one for the parliament and another one for tax raising powers. It was well understood in Scotland that Forsyth was opposed to devolution, and that his plan was to undermine it. However this obstacle was overcome by the Scottish electorate which voted for the additional power.

It is said that when pressed to identify her greatest legacy to the Conservatives, Margaret Thatcher claimed that it was the development of 'New Labour'. This may, or may not be true, but it does seem to be a very astute observation for someone with the limited political vision of Thatcher to make.

What is beyond doubt, is that New Labour picked up the baton of neo-liberalism from the Thatcherites and carried it forward within the UK establishment

CHAPTER 5

Unscrupulous Banking

The Debt Crisis

For many people the events of 2008 and the dramatic and catastrophic failure of the banking system all over the capitalist world, were a major shock and complete surprise.

We watched in horror at the powerful implications on the UK economy of the debt crisis as it began to unfold and people wanted desperately to know what it was and what caused it?

Why did this financial crisis arise and spread so suddenly and rapidly like the Black Death, right across America, Britain, Europe and other countries trading with these blocks and using the Dollar, Pound or Euro? Was there some explanation for this? It seemed to have hit governments, economists, journalists, and other professionals, with as much surprise as the general public.

We have since been told it is a *debt* problem, but let's think about that. If a group of people dealing and trading with each other find a debt issue, it will have certain obvious characteristics:

It will have an effect on some, but not all, because if some owe money they must owe it to others, so if some are in debt others must be in surplus.

It will have built up slowly over time and will have become progressively more obvious, because some will be borrowing, and others will be lending, and all transactions will have been meticulously recorded. So debts never come suddenly, they always build up over time.

This debt crisis appears to be quite different. If we take account of the people at the centre of the crisis in the UK their stories are quite dramatic.

Alistair Darling, who was Chancellor of the Exchequer at the time, claims that Fred Goodwin, the Chief Executive of RBS, called at his house in Edinburgh at the weekend out of the blue. Fred told him that if the UK Government did not find many billions of pounds within days to hand over to the bank, then the cash machines would close down, and one of the largest banks in the world would collapse.

Is this true? Is that what really happened?

We now know that the Chancellor and the Prime Minister did hand over billions of taxpayer's money to RBS, and to other banks, and took a number of other actions using taxpayer's money to support the financial system.

We also know it was all in great haste, there being little time to draw up a proper agreement or exit strategy, or protocol as to how this money was to be used. Or so it appears, because Fred Goodwin took a few million out of the government's rescue package for his personal severance and pension settlement and jumped ship leaving the problems behind.

The rescued banks then resumed business as usual, and carried on paying bonuses to their top staff from the government hand-out. Is this version of events credible?

If every country in the capitalist world is in debt, who is in surplus and demanding repayment? Furthermore, why did no one realise that a gigantic debt was building up, and warn the government about this before it happened. The Labour government, in the Financial Services and Markets Act 2000, had set up the Financial Services Authority (FSA). Its sole purpose was to regulate and investigate the banks and financial services in the UK.

The FSA was accountable to the UK Treasury, where Alistair Darling was in charge, so why did he not know there was a major crisis brewing in the banks until Fred Goodwin chapped on his door in Edinburgh? After all, there had been a crisis in Northern Rock some months earlier. This just could not be credible if the banks and regulatory authority were functioning as they should.

We all know from personal experience how normal banking works. We go to the bank for the big costly items in our lives, the house, car, weddings etc; we sign an agreement and we get a loan. The agreement must be signed before we get a penny of this money, and in the agreement it is made clear how soon the loan must be repaid and how much interest we will pay. Business banking is on similar lines, although loans are often secured by putting other assets forward as collateral. So in general normal banking is a very safe, simple and lucrative business.

It is fairly obvious that if banks were suddenly threatened with a domino style collapse, caused by massive losses and urgently needing immediate bail-out, then they were involved in something very different from normal banking.

All banks are required to qualify for the privilege of a government charter, granted in terms of the Banking Acts. If they breech that charter surely that should not imply collapse of the entire system.

The banks and financial services were indeed doing something other than traditional banking, and had literally been encouraged to do so by the neo-liberal light touch regulation as introduced by Thatcher and Reagan.

The terms of their original charters to provide collateralised credit to the public were cast aside as:-

- they took control of the national money supply from government
- they devised new financial 'products' known collectively as derivatives which were classed and treated as assets for trading within financial markets which when challenged proved to be largely worthless
- they used the money of depositors and the guarantee of the taxpayer to finance the trading of these so-called assets

All these matters and their implications are comprehensively dealt with in Part Two.

It was not normal banking arrangements which created the financial eruption, it is these shadowy activities which caused the crisis, and the banks are still playing these same games. The magma lake is filling up again under the UK economy, and it will happen again, and we will have another eruption. It is merely a matter of time.

The widespread claim that we, the community, caused the crisis by borrowing too much is just not true. The claim that we are collectively responsible and are in it together is not true. The suggestion that spending, on public health and education, or care of the elderly, caused this crisis is not true. The irrational dogma that austerity and unemployment will resolve this problem is not true.

The banks and financial services industry in the USA, UK, and Europe, alone caused this crisis, and the current huge increase in Government debts in Britain, Europe and the USA is largely the result of tax-payers having to bail-out the banks. That is where this additional debt came from.

In Westminster today the present Tory/Liberal Coalition blame the previous Labour administration for the debt while Labour blames them for mishandling the problem. Both sides ignore the obvious - it was the banks and their extracurricular activities which triggered the crisis.

Whilst the cause of the collapse is now beginning to be understood, the explanation of why it was allowed to happen, remains shrouded in mystery. What on the face of it appears to have been criminal fraud on a massive and worldwide scale is being accepted by world leaders as beyond the reach of the forces of international law and order. It appears that the entire Western monetary system is in the hands of a super-mafia.

However, if that were the case, and there was really nothing anyone could do about it, then there would be no point in us drawing it to attention. We (the authors) believe that people can determine their own destiny if they set their minds to it, and we hope that writing these words can help people to do that.

Let us return for a moment to the question of who are all these countries indebted to? Who lent the USA, the UK, most European countries, and several others around the world, all this money which they have to pay back? Who indeed has such large amounts of money to lend?

The answer is that these colossal sums of money were lent out by banks, which are effectively controlled by a small number of mega rich individuals who own or effectively control vast amounts of the assets in the capitalist world. This group is not large in number, only a few thousand, but they are immensely wealthy and powerful. They control the banking system and most of the major corporations, they control the financial markets, they own the media and they are over represented in our legislatures by dint of well paid lobbyists and via the funding of political parties.

It is to the banking institutions, under the control of this small financial elite, to whom countries ultimately owe their national debts.

It is this group which wants the ordinary people to pay for their country's debts. It is they who insist on austerity because they want to redress the balance of income distribution further towards the wealthy, and they want more publicly owned assets in their hands.

The media agree with this because they own the media. The money markets agree with them because they own the money markets. The banks ditto. It is a circular argument.

That shadowy group known as the core of the Establishment agrees that the mega-rich need to be richer, and that the rest of us should cut back our consumption in order to pay for it. That is the human face of this arithmetical problem.

The Establishment, unfortunately, also includes the economists and academics in the capitalist world who mainly adhere to an economic system which makes this obscene distribution of income possible.

It is an ideology which will become increasingly oppressive until the entire monetary system implodes. This malevolent force will continue to dominate for as long as it remains unchallenged.

Let us therefore start to build our challenge by returning briefly to Adam Smith's ideas. In 1849 an obscure German Doctor of Philosophy, Dr Karl Friedrich Marx came from Paris to live in poverty in London. He managed to support himself by writing for an American newspaper, and he relied on his close friend Friedrich Engels, whose family were wealthy factory owners in Manchester. Engels was also originally from Germany and knew Marx from his years in Paris.

Marx was very impressed by Adam Smith and studied his economic ideas carefully. What Marx liked in particular about Smith, was Smith's scientific approach, which allowed his readers to check out his theoretical predictions in the real economy over a period of time. So Marx did exactly that in relation to Smith's work nearly a century later.

Adam Smith had tried to examine and explain every aspect of economic activity and he analysed each aspect of the subject to see how it worked. In doing this, Smith had decided that there were three basic *elements* required in order to produce wealth, and he identified these as what we would now call: labour, natural resources and capital. His claim was that with these elements, and only with these 'elements' at hand, can wealth be created.

Smith was watching very early forms of capitalism in Glasgow in the 1770's, and at that time the early capitalists were not wealthy men and needed to borrow capital from the aristocrats. Smith did not call this 'capital', he called it 'rent'. (Nowadays some in Scotland still use this term 'rent' to describe interest paid on money borrowed from the bank).

Smith had explained how the capitalist method of production, while vastly increasing total production and total labour, was also making labour more productive for very good reasons. He predicted that labour would increase its productivity and that the amount of labour per unit of production would fall. He also predicted, for similar good sound reasons, that while total use of natural resources would continue to rise, that again the amount per unit of production would fall.

Now in Smith's time the labour cost of production would have been relatively high, say something like 80% of the total, and natural resources would have been around say 19%, while capital was almost non-existent, probably less that 1%. Smith therefore never bothered to look at capital as a proportion of new production.

Marx looked at these predictions and did the calculations. They proved that Smith was right. Labour as a percentage of the cost of each new unit of production was falling very significantly, and so was the cost of natural resources. So Smith was right, this was a factual observation with huge implications for human development.

Since production is wealth, it meant that if people continued to organise production along these lines they could continue to produce wealth with less labour and less natural resources per unit. This was good news and suggested a prosperous future for mankind.

However there was one sour note. When he examined the evidence, Marx noted that while both labour and natural resources were continuing to fall per unit of production, 'capital' was in fact rising per unit, so in the 1870's, one hundred years after Smith's observations, the figures of cost per unit of production might seem more likely to be labour 69%, natural resources 16% and capital 15%. So Marx turned his attention to capital; what was it, and why did it increasingly account for more as production increased?

Marx was fascinated by this subject and eventually wrote a three volume work '*Das Kapital*' on the subject in which he looked again at Smith's *elements*[1] He used Smith's own methodology, and Smith's work on value, where Smith had identified 'labour input' as the major factor which determined value as opposed to price. It was from this work of Smith's that Marx developed the concept of 'surplus value'.

Marx then decided that there were indeed only two 'elements' - Labour and Natural Resources. Capital, he claimed, was not a separate element but was indeed merely consolidated labour. It was labour preserved in a transferable form.

Furthermore, as Marx pointed out one *element*[2] cannot be constructed out of other *elements;* by definition. Labour and capital, without natural resources cannot make wealth; natural resources and capital can't make wealth without labour; but labour and natural resources can make capital and therefore can make wealth. Capital therefore, is not an element of production, and need not be rewarded as such.

Capitalist economics however had always been based upon the principle that all three elements of production must get a reward per unit, as they are all necessary elements of production, which is directly in line with Adam Smith's initial view on this.

Marx contends that this belief has created a situation where capital is being paid per unit, and was already becoming an ever increasing *burden* on the cost of production, rather than a fundamental *element*.

This process has serious implications which Marx noted and identified. It means that 'capital' receiving a return per unit of production, and an increasing return, each new unit as the capital impute per unit grows means that over time capital will demand a larger and larger share of new production.

---

1.   It was labour preserved in a transferable form. In other words anything which an economist would define as capital is just consolidated labour. We can test this and find that it is valid. For example a factory building which would be defined as capital represents the labour plus materials which went into it; the same applies to a tractor or any other manufacture. The same conclusion even holds good in respect of money borrowed as working capital from savings earned in the past as the fruits of someone else's labour. It would not apply of course to credit borrowed from a bank. (This differentiation is important and examined in great detail in Part Two).

2.   In this context, as in physics & philosophy, an element is basic and cannot be further divided into component parts

Clearly if capital claims a larger and larger share per unit of production, then labour and natural resources have to survive on a smaller and smaller share. That in turn implies a redistribution of income from labour to capital. That simply means that those who contribute the labour, i.e. most of us, will have to make do with an ever smaller share of the benefits of production.

Marx also considered that over time owners of capital would compete against other capitalists and against labour to demand ever higher returns on their investments; while these investments grew as a proportion of new production – indeed their economic theory saw this drive for a return per unit as the very engine of wealth creation. That translates to what some call the growth imperative today – the force which favours cheap labour and imports over local industry because they make a higher short term profit.

In free market terms this is the sole driver of 'growth' because it externalises all the social costs and all considerations of sustainability

It is irresponsible short- termism which feeds on the greed of the already rich and powerful; it is the 'last man standing' philosophy which has driven us into the box canyon of the present financial crisis.

Marx described this pressure as leading to the 'falling rate of profit' which we might today describe as 'a rising rate of debt'; where the demand for a high return on capital, is met by increasing debt, rather than real resources. So levels of notional debt borrowed at interest escalate exponentially.

This debt is accepted as a claim upon future production. In today's terms this relates to the debt/GDP ratio which in the UK represents a level of debt well in excess of next year's total GDP, (total income of everyone in the country). To keep this system going, we will all need to live on the bare minimum for survival, while we build up huge mountains of notional debt upon which our children will pay the interest via the tax system to the children of the mega rich – *reductio ad absurdum.*

Moving from theory to practice, can this trend be interpreted to provide a basis for policy making? We keep finding new ways to improve production methods. Our objective every time is to find a new technology which takes less labour effort and which improves on the use of materials. We keep doing this, and getting better at it. The way we do it is to use more capital, normally in the form of machines or gadgets which help us to make things. That is exactly what Marx was talking about in the 1870's.

This kind of progress in production techniques is not a problem for the economic system itself. The problem arises with the distribution of the rewards for each *element.*

The idea that capital needs to get the same reward as labour, and needs a return per unit of production is the problem, because if you do this you will be paying more and more for capital as production methods advance. But of course capital is an inanimate object. It has no need for such an immense reward and has no means of using it. It is not the capital which wants and is seeking reward, it is the people who claim ownership of the capital.

Is this ownership a legitimate claim when the vast bulk of this capital is found to be notional debt issued by the private banking system, but ultimately guaranteed by the taxpayer? And is the taxpayer not today's physical manifestation of Marx's Labour? Virtually all money is now in the form of electronic bank credit which in the final analysis does not belong to the bank but to the taxpayer. The bank is merely the agent of the taxpayer.

Of course there are almost as many interpretations of Marx's theory of 'falling rate of profit' as there are scholars researching the subject, but this book is not about economic theory, what is clear is that there can be no disputing that production requires less and less labour as each day brings greater automation. The vast bulk of the capital element of Smith's original factors of production is not privately owned – it is the credit of the taxpayer.

The corollary of this interpretation is that the trillions of bank credit in circulation is not the property of the banks or their shareholders, but of the taxpayers. The system is an inanimate mechanism, but the bankers who operate it grow ever richer on the interest, whilst the taxpayers grow ever poorer as the debt in the system rises exponentially.

The system is irrational and unsustainable. Its collapse is merely postponed by the bailout of the banks and the ongoing printing of money in a futile attempt to stabilise their balance sheets – and as always, funded by the taxpayer.

The further development of this thesis, is at the core of Part Two, but let us return to the matter of trends to assist in economic policy making.

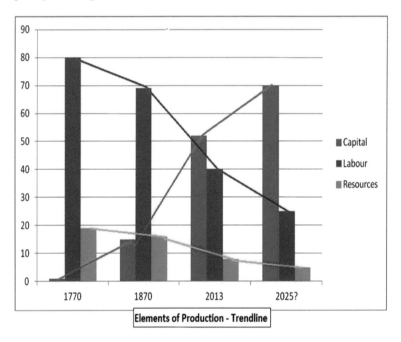

Elements of Production - Trendline

The illustration represents trends in the ratio of elements over time in production. The coloured blocks do not represent any specific values, but are approximations of subjective observations. A trend does not require numbers any more than the statement, 'the seasons will become progressively warmer or cooler as the Earth mover closer to or away from the Sun', requires us to know the exact temperature at any specific point on the surface of the Sun or the Earth.

A motor car will have a different elemental ratio from that of a mile of motorway; a bottle of coke clearly has a small labour content compared to the services of a window cleaner. Reference is made in economics to capital intensive, or labour intensive production systems. Again the specific ratios which inform the elements are not cogent to the trend.

In 1770 the vast bulk of the population worked in agriculture. Food and clothing would be the main products, and capital would be minimal or non- existent. By 1870 the UK is well into the industrial revolution and the mills are driven by steam engines. (**NB** the latter also comprising labour and natural resources.)

However, there remains a significant agricultural community. Merchants and international trade are becoming important participants in the productive cycle, and banks are becoming established as providers of capital – although with the important proviso that all money and credit is still predicated upon gold and silver. That means the capital is largely 'real' in terms of savings and investment.

Today we know that all money is now bank credit, and that financial services and debt play dominant roles in unwinding imports, and what little productive industry remains.

2013 is dominated by capital in the form of debt. We may not know the exact proportions but something over half must be a modest assessment.

That is sufficient to connect a few dots and detect a trend. So what are the implications of this trend? Clearly if developments in robotics and automation continue in this way, and as we learn to use natural resources more efficiently, for example using renewables and recycled raw materials, it is easy to see that labour and natural resources will continue to fall as a proportion of the whole, while capital will continue to rise per unit of production.

When considering labour as an element, it should be remembered that this represents all incomes earned in the course of production and distribution – from the office junior or apprentice to the most senior executives and directors, in fact the 99.9% of society.

All would be entitled to a smaller and smaller share of new production (*as illustrated by the graph on page 61*).

Conversely 'capital' in this context is manifested in the financial institutions – primarily the banks. The capital is in fact the debt generated by the debt-money system. It is 'systemic debt', and only the 0.1% elite control this system and are able to print their own incomes. Although their personal wealth is miniscule in relation to the systemic debt which is the total money supply, they control the process and reap the rewards.

What you are reading here is not new, it is just being presented in a new context – that of the worldwide debt and banking crisis.

The theory of the elements of production is widely accepted across the economics spectrum; the main differences of opinion occurring thereafter in designing the best means of achieving real wealth across the whole community. We know this because it has been done before and we need to isolate the financial problem which stands in the way of achieving this again.

Scotland's young people deserve a better future than is currently on offer from Westminster and the Bank of England. It is wicked and inhumane in this day and age that an entire generation is being saddled with unemployment and financial hardship in sacrifice to an economic dogma imposed by a tiny elitist minority.

Politicians such as Johann Lamont seem to believe that accepting austerity is merely acknowledging economic necessity and is unavoidable. They appear to believe that people who resist this are not only economically illiterate but are selfish and weak.

We are the 'something for nothing society', and need to wake up to the importance of austerity and cuts in public investment. They attempt to put their own ignorance and incompetence upon the shoulders of their own community, rather than face up to the obvious.

It is not the people and their aspirations which is the problem; it is the impossibility of satisfying the insatiable demands of the monetary system we have unwittingly unleashed, and the greed and self-interest of the privileged few who drive it.

CHAPTER 6

Present State of the UK Economy

The Outlook for the UK Economy

Any review of the UK economy is not going to be a laugh a minute, and when we come to its future prospects there isn't much to cheer us up. Other than in times of war, the UK has never achieved the productive wealth of Germany – not because of weak management or militant unions, but because London has always been more interested in making money rather than goods and services. No matter the Mansion House speeches and the superficial glitz of the much trumpeted financial sector, at the end of the day the figures don't lie

So after that all too brief spell of full employment and reconstruction immediately after the war, what were the economic dividends of all that blood, sweat and tears? Well, take a look at these numbers.

With a total population of 62.74 million, the UK has a national debt of £1,377.4 billion (1st quarter 2013). That represents 90.7% of its GDP, and demands annual interest payments of £43 billion. This debt is rising by around £2.3 billion per week and is predicted to rise to 95% of GDP by the end of this year, and to be 98.7% of UK GDP by 2014. By the time of the referendum the UK will owe the full value of everything it makes in the following year to the money lenders.

You probably skipped over those familiar numbers with a sigh. But if you were suddenly told that you were personally £22,000 in debt and that the interest rate was 5% pa and £685 a year and that your bank account was paying out a direct debit to the government of £57.08 per month you might pay more attention. If you also had a couple of young children your direct debit would be £171.24 a month, and oh yes, you had nothing to show for it – you would probably be pretty miffed and pay more attention. Well, prepare to be miffed, because that's exactly what every man, woman and child in the UK owes as their personal share of the National Debt, and your earnings for the whole of next year are mortgaged to the system.

Doesn't apply to you? Every time you buy something in a shop you pay VAT of 20%; on each litre of fuel you pay over 80 pence in tax- so think again. Our message in this book is to get you involved in asking why this country is going down the tubes, because it certainly is.

There are two main reasons, first the banks and the City of London issue and manage our money system for their personal enrichment, and second, the government, no matter its political stripe, condones it. There is no remote prospect of any change in that situation, and as a result the economy is stagnant, the prospect is for austerity, and even at best, stunted growth followed by more austerity. Even if you are on benefit you still pay your direct debit and prices will continue to soar.

What about selling off some state assets built up by the Attlee government? Sorry, but they're all gone: the mines, the railways, electricity generation and distribution, gas production and distribution etc. All went under the privatisation hammer for the benefit of the consumer and taxpayer, *or* so the Tories told us at the time. Mrs Thatcher at least stopped short of selling off the Royal Mail. No such qualms deter her successors though...

Mmmm... The family silver has all gone then. What about putting our factories back on their feet and making things to export like we used to do when Britain was the Workshop of the World? No, no there's no money for that, don't you understand that we're broke? Besides we couldn't possibly compete with the Chinese, or the Germans or anyone else for that matter – our wages are already far too high... *so Westminster tells us.*

"But Mr. Osborne, what about some shipbuilding, we can still build aircraft carriers and atomic submarines – how about building some container ships and cruise liners for wealthy foreigners who seem to be able to manage their affairs better than us?"

"No! No, it's the same problem. No money to re-equip our civil yards, and the old skills are long gone. Look, will you just shut up and write to your MP if you want to complain. You can leave it to us to keep the wheels turning in the City of London. Unfortunately, I haven't the time to explain to you how that works in your interests because it's very complicated and you probably wouldn't understand anyway. Good afternoon!"

Not too unlikely a scenario perhaps, but what about that City stuff – they do seem to make a lot of money there.... perhaps we might find someone else to tell us about that? Preferably someone who is not paid by the banks or employed in this financial business, and please, please not those professors of economics from the ivory towers of academia who argue their abstruse theories and then leave us none the wiser. Is there someone from the real world of work and the gritty reality of making and building things?

Well here we are, and half way through setting up our stall. If you have stuck with us this far we can provide answers and ideas which are seldom aired on the media. For those who seek more information about independence then this is where to be.

The UK can successfully export financial services and financial products. Indeed the UK is now like one of its own super banks. It has international assets and liabilities, centred in the city of London, just like a super bank with assets and of course matching liabilities, now over 700% of the UK's GDP.

Certainly, this huge sector earns interest and dividends in foreign markets, and plays a powerful and increasing role in Britain's international trade, and it has been doubling in size every 9 years. In terms of economic success that ticks most of the boxes – but not all. What about sustainability and stability? There is a major problem here which is looming in the shadows.

If the UK economy is like a super bank, and operates like that, is it not possible, even likely, that it will be affected by the same problems, and suddenly find that it has a lot of toxic paper assets and therefore vulnerable to the same domino collapse pattern which may turn into another huge liability on the UK taxpayer again?

That is the problem with financial assets – we can see the huge office blocks of Canary Wharf and Wall Street as clearly as the factory buildings of Vauxhall in Luton, or Aggreko in Dumbarton. The difference is we can see the cars coming out of Luton and the huge generators coming out of Dumbarton bound for every corner on Earth. What comes from Canary Wharf is a mystery to most people and of little value to society in general.

Just what does go on inside these glass pyramids occupies a chapter in Part Two. Of course no one in their right mind would suggest that the UK economy could be holed below the waterline and is slowly sinking. It is outrageous, totally unacceptable.

It would be politically incorrect to suggest that the UK economy is on the skids. We do not go in for predictions, we are only concerned with identifying how the system operates; but a similar state of mind pervaded those aboard a large liner back in 1912.

For the first half hour after the Titanic hit the iceberg, no one, other than in secret and in whispers, suggested that the ship would sink. Everyone knew the Titanic was unsinkable, the very idea that a lump of floating ice could sink this magnificent ship was thought to be pure nonsense.

Science however proved to be unimpressed by the myth of the Titanic's famed unsinkability. The ship sank because too many compartments were flooding. If it had been one less it would have survived, but the reality was that it would sink. It was a mathematical certainty.

If we are told that the UK economy will recover from this present difficulty we need more than blind faith, or bland assurances that it will not get worse. We need to know upon what basis this recovery can be achieved. Where are the tools and ingredients to build upon?

The NO Campaign demands details about an independent Scotland's economic performance in the future as though this was commonplace. They could just as legitimately ask about the future of the UK economy's debt mountain and how it will be dealt with. That is a more pertinent and more appropriate question.

However many people have been asking this more pertinent question of our 'leaders' in Westminster, their response is now nearly six years overdue, bringing the words of Lewis Carroll to mind.

> *"O Oysters", said the Carpenter,*
> *"You've had a pleasant run!*
> *Shall we be trotting home again?"*
> *But answer came there none-*
> *And this was scarcely odd, because*
> *They'd eaten every one*

Political Style of Management

In spite of all the doom and gloom, it is not inevitable that the UK economy will collapse, indeed if the Westminster Government were to adopt a Keynesian recovery strategy and invest in industry in order to bring the unemployed, and underemployed in the UK into production, this could significantly increase GDP and reduce public expenditure on benefits and subsidies.

Westminster claims the economy will recover if we just put blind faith in the free market. Yet they are determined to pursue austerity and cut public investment. How on earth can inactivity and unemployment possibly stop the rot let alone rebuild a viable economy? It is the rationale of the paper shufflers in the Treasury, the Bank of England and Canary Wharf, but it will not reverse the trend, and there can be little of greater economic importance than keeping everyone gainfully employed - that is one of the main planks of our independence platform.

Exactly how this recovery will happen is not explained so let us try and guess what they are thinking. The private sector of the economy is not investing any more than the public sector is, because with falling real incomes there is a fall in effective demand.

This Government is refusing to use its position to invest in line with the Keynesian model, and sitting on its hands waiting like Mr. Micawber for 'something to turn up'. Meantime, there are almost 8% unemployed, probably as many 'underemployed' on part time contracts, and a further one million on 'zero-hours contracts'.

This latest wheeze of the zero-hour's contract is a real step back for working people. This is reminiscent of the bad old days of the twenties and thirties when the dockers had to stand around the dock gates waiting for some of their number to be called to work on a day to day basis. They too had no secure income and no rights or benefits.

All this makes good policy for a government which believes that cheap labour makes for a competitive economy and, of course, if you are on zero hours you do not figure on the unemployment register - another plus for an administration more concerned with numbers.

This economic policy is a disaster for small companies as well as for employees. A Keynesian type revival would be of great benefit to domestic business in the UK. These principles again are not new, just overwhelmed by multi-national corporations.

'Small is beautiful', is a short book by E.F. Schumacher, the British economist who champions people, small organisations and community enterprise. Its philosophy is not spoken of in the corridors of power and big business in Westminster. The sentiments might however be more familiar at Holyrood where the seeds of Keynesian principles might well find fertile ground.

An independent Scotland would be a life-line to local businesses. Lively and innovative commercial activity is vital to the healthy growth of all models of small successful economies.

They require nurturing by government, and although a leavening of big business is desirable, it should never be seen as more than part of a well balanced whole.

In smaller countries like Scandinavia, where wages are relatively high, then effective demand in the domestic market is strong and sustained. This is reflected in a wide variety of equally sustainable local businesses which tend to rely on the domestic market. Sometimes the macro-economists who think in global terms miss the point that it is the people who comprise the economy, as well as providing the work-force, they also provide the effective demand for the domestic market.

That is the kind of macro-management which dominates the thinking of most economists in Westminster. They perceive multinationals and big business as the hope and salvation of the British economy. It may seem like that on the twentieth floor of an office block on Canary Wharf, or to the converted Mr Vince Cable in his offices at The Ministry for Business, Innovation and Skills.

The Scots can keep going to the polls to vote for Westminster MPs until they are blue in the face, but they will not get business policies appropriate to Scotland.

We can only conclude that Westminster is not working, certainly for Scotland, and indeed much of the North of England. The Scots however are fortunate in having this upcoming referendum, offering the opportunity for a management buy-out, and to run their own business in a way that suits them.

The Democratic Process

It is a long time since Scots shared in a Westminster government which reflected their hopes and aspirations. The prospect of a truly democratic and egalitarian society for the UK dimmed fifty years ago, and dropped below the horizon when the very idea of fairness itself became a victim to New Labour. The UK is now a poor reflection of America, where it is hard to detect any meaningful difference between the dominant political parties.

The collective noun, 'The Establishment', has been used several times in previous chapters and will be used several more times in the next few paragraphs. Perhaps it is time to be a little more specific. The Establishment is a hierarchy of power and authority and nothing to do with democracy, because we did not vote for them. Perhaps the bankers voted for the chairman of the British Bankers Association and the directors and CEOs of Big Business voted for the Chairman of the Confederation of British Industry (CBI). There was probably a vote for the Leader of the House of Lords, but the election didn't make the pages of the Scotsman or the Daily Record. Come to think of it no one voted for any of the Lords and Ladies either, and if you think the BBC is an impartial instrument of democracy then you haven't been listening carefully.

The Establishment, is of course just a label for the ruling economic, social and cultural administration, but this fairly wide group which changes its composition is dominated by an inner small core which does not change frequently, this group is the ruling elite, and they do not stand for election.

The Great and the Good of our Establishment are to be found inhabiting the Public Inquiries and Royal Commissions which are appointed from time to time to discreetly smooth over any unforeseen aberration which might threaten to disturb the peace and good order of the Realm. Finally there is the facade of the Commons Committees which administer a public school spanking to any member of the Establishment caught by the public eye in *flagrante delicto*. This is inevitably followed by a return to business as usual. Thus this elitist institution ensures its own survival and our unique style of British democracy.

The New Labour Party, which inherited an enviable reputation from those who led it in the past, and which still basks in their political inheritance of the NHS and the welfare system, became part of The Establishment when it conveniently forgot its history and mutated into a mirror image of the Conservative Party – only the rhetoric was different. Both parties share power as a result of elections which are designed to exclude mavericks, although, there is a superficial tolerance of wishy-washy liberals who bend with the wind from whatever direction.

The resultant administration enjoys nominal power entirely at the discretion of the British Establishment whose representatives encourage all the external panoply of democracy at the Palace of Westminster, but ensure, with the most subtle diplomacy that money can buy, that the United Kingdom continues to be ruled in their best interests.

It is recognition of this powerful reality which paralyses political parties in the Westminster system. They know there is a strict limit to what can be done, or even discussed in politics, within the parameters set by the elite and maintained by their organs in the media and elsewhere. This has resulted in all political parties in the UK being the same in terms of economic policy, and makes them desperate to display some difference in style and perception.

Too many politicians in the UK today are all produced out of the same mould. At one time Labour MPs would be ex-miners, dockers, teachers, lawyers, engineers, and a range of other jobs, professions and life experiences. They are now the same as every other party, i.e. they come straight from university to be political advisors and researchers, and then are selected as MPs.

So what is all this political advice about? The Attlee government seemed to manage well enough without any of them. Political advisors are today not about politics, they are about winning elections.

Politics has been quietly abandoned by our politicians. The elite no longer allow them to practice the art of the possible. Put another way, there is no future for a dedicated politician with principles and a burning ambition to improve the living conditions of his constituents and to build a better society. There is a better game in Westminster town – that of supporting the interests of 'The Establishment', and winning elections. If your politics are the same as those of your competitor across the floor, then you need to compete in terms of your television appeal and style – forget substance, and conscience, and of course your constituents, until just before the next election...

No professional New Labour politician will talk in any depth about the Attlee government's achievements or Keynesian economics. To do so would destroy their career prospects as a 'sound' member of the Club. Then again, the electoral system in Westminster is totally skewed and could not be better designed to prevent potentially controversial ideas breaking the surface.

Then the first past the post system further ensures that a political party must have the support of the Establishment to make any kind of showing at the polls. That in turn would require the support of the media, which is, of course, owned by the Establishment.

Let's be brutally frank! Democracy as a vehicle of real political change in the UK is dead, or at least it is in intensive care and unlikely to recover. Democracy itself has been 'bought' by the all powerful elite who run the UK. The unionist politicians we see every day urging us to accept austerity so that the economy can recover, are nothing but bought and sold puppets of an unseen puppet master who pulls their strings. These people are unable to discuss political freedom with us - they would not know what it means.

CHAPTER 7

Monetisation of Society

In this final chapter of this part we cut through the jargon, and the technical language which has disguised the most blatant misappropriation of community resources built up and maintained by the UK taxpayer over many years.

If we learn from this experience then it should serve as a warning against an Independent Scotland falling into a similar trap.

Monetisation

Monetisation is a financial term meaning converting an asset into money – selling your house is monetisation, or taking your accumulated junk along to a car boot sale.

Money has always been an important fact of life for all of us, but the monetisation of government policy is a more recent development which has come to dominate the decision making process. The change was accelerated under Thatcherism, when managing the monetary system was transferred from being a responsibility of government into private hands, which led directly to the deregulation of the banks and the unprecedented growth of public debt.

The social impact of privatisation on the currency has been enormous and without historical precedent. It has been the driving force behind far more privatisations than will be recalled by the present generation. It is difficult to steal a locomotive, or a post office, or a fresh water reservoir, or an airport; but if you monetise it first then it's easy.

Burma Oil was founded in Glasgow in 1886 and went on to become BP, the fifth largest energy company in the world.

It lost its main assets in Burma during WW2, and the remainder due to nationalisation there in 1963. In 1965 it was the first company to strike oil in the North Sea. In 1974 the company made huge losses on its tanker fleet and was rescued by the taxpayer, and was nationalised in 1974.

During 1977/1987, at the height of the North Sea oil boom, the Westminster government privatised the company. Just imagine the personal fortunes made from this sell-off alone and the value to the national economy of having a national oil company like this today.

That however was just the beginning of selling off the British taxpayer's assets. There were so many huge businesses sold off over some thirty years that they cannot be listed here, but take a look at the 150 names in Appendix 4 and then contemplate how this once rich country has become one and a half trillion pounds in debt, the one per cent of the population millionaires, while 99% are still wondering what happened to them.

Monetisation of Government

Well, what happened was this. Most of these national assets were substantial companies and buying their shares, even at knock down prices, was beyond the average private sector entrepreneur. So Big Business went to their colleagues at the bank and borrowed billions to buy out these monopolies from the state. The banks had the assets as collateral, and Big Business owned the shares and all the profits into the distant future. They achieved their free market objective, the banks conjured up the wherewithal from thin air, and Big Business became even bigger. Everyone was happy.

These industries were slimmed down and shed significant jobs. Many were sold to foreign investors for a quick buck, but did the consumer bills drop? Well you know the answer to that question.

These household names, Scottish Hydro, SSEB, and Scottish Gas, all the national utilities sold off as 'inefficient' services, which would be much more competitive and save us great wedges of cash following privatisation. Aye, that'll be right then, but there's more.

PFI Devices

Have you any idea of the money made by those 'in the know' out of PFI – the Private Finance Initiative? Respected economists Jim and Margaret Cuthbert found that:

"In Scotland alone, PFI deals in operation or signed cover capital expenditure of £5.1 billion, almost all under Labour. Further £1.7 billion future deals are in preparation".

They were able to uncover details of one example – "a hospital project in England with a capital cost of just under £70 million. To finance the building the consortium borrowed over £60m from banks, at an interest rate of just over 6 per cent: the consortium itself provided almost £10m subordinate debt for the project, for which it received a more generous 15 per cent, and the consortium also put in an equity stake of £1,000: (no, we have not misread the decimal point: we genuinely mean one thousand pounds). The project shows the classic signs of inappropriate indexation, with the senior debt being paid off quickly, and hence senior debt charges declining rapidly - but with the whole unitary charge being indexed over the full thirty year life of the project at 3 per cent per annum. As a result, the projected returns to the consortium are eye-watering: the £1,000 equity input is projected to earn dividends totalling to more than £50m. Taking account of projected undistributed reserves at the end of the project, the consortium's own financial projections indicate that the consortium is expecting to reap a cash return of more than £90m in total on its investment, (by way of subordinate debt and equity), of less than £10m".

On our own doorstep, the new Edinburgh Royal Infirmary was estimated to come in at around £180 million. PPI/PPP was to add up to £1080 million over a 30 year period, and even at the end of that period it still would belong to the private consortia.

So the process is like the skilled operator with sleight of hand inviting you to bet on which cup the ball is under. You should not be obliged to guess, because it's your money in the first place... and when you are told that it's OK because it's a not for profit game – then be even more wary, you are dealing with a serious confidence trickster.

Privatisation of Public Assets

You will no doubt have a school near you built under PFI, where the skilled tradesmen who actually built it, and the teachers who teach in it, are described as fortunate to have a steady job in these difficult times.

The buildings were however not built to employ anyone. Their primary purpose was to enrich the banks which lent the finance, and the big construction firms who negotiated the contract, without the need for a competitive tender.

Then there was the sale of council houses, variously described as a Thatcherite ploy to win conservative votes in England and to undermine the principle of social housing and stopping any more council houses being built. This was a different kind of privatisation, whereby a million council houses were sold off to sitting tenants at a discount of 30/50% of valuation.

A number of councils have simply transferred their residual housing stock to housing associations which were able to operate a much easier business model.

It works like this. The housing association receives the stock of houses free of charge. It then borrows tens of millions from the banks to refurbish them. It sells off some of them and rents out the balance. Provided the income covers the salaries and overheads of this 'social enterprise', everyone is happy. The bank is happy because it has a safe loan, out at 6%, and the collateral of refurbished and sellable houses; the council is happy not to have the maintenance bill for a rundown housing stock; the private housing market gets a boost – once again everyone's a winner. Except the poor old taxpayer who provided the money for the council houses in the first place, and which now have been kindly donated to the association.

Few people take into account that the money to build these houses was borrowed from the Public Loans Board – just another name for the national debt. As with all Westminster wheezes, the banks win and the public pays.

Since the passing of the Attlee government, Westminster has always been about big business, high finance and the City of London. Everywhere else was an appendage, a nuisance to be tolerated as a necessary overhead to be maintained at minimum cost. That is Great Britain Limited.

It is an enterprise run for the benefit of the shareholders, who live mainly in the home counties, and employ the best accountants to ensure they pay little or no tax. The law of the land is carefully crafted to favour big business over the self-employed and the smaller enterprises, which employ the majority of the population and pay most of the taxes.

Westminster projects a public image of financial prudence, but do you ever get the feeling that this is a type of government dedicated to its own special interest group rather than the common weal? Huge sums of taxpayer's money are allocated to unemployment benefits and subsidies, to assist the finances of the poorly paid, the part timers, and the unfortunates of the zero hours contracts, and the futile efforts of agencies engaged in job creation and fancy schemes to get people back to work. This is all funded with taxpayer's money. It seems almost too obvious that it would be better all round to invest this money in the creation of public assets which would create a demand among employers to take on workers to meet a natural demand for labour and apprentices.

Externalisation

There is an explanation, and it is a skill highly valued in Big Business circles. It is called *externalisation.*

This is a universal mechanism whereby the normally accepted costs of doing business are unloaded on to someone else. When ATH Resources in Fife went into liquidation it left behind a scarred landscape and a polluted water table to be cleared up by the Coal Authority.

The operators of rail services are subsidized by Network Rail which runs the tracks and stations.

The tobacco industry does not contribute to the NHS, and when Westminster privatized British Nuclear Fuels and the electricity companies, they conveniently left behind the estimated £70bn cost of cleaning up to the National Decontamination Authority.

Now consider the privatisation of our public utilities. They were all transferred with billions of pounds worth of network infrastructure, rails and stations, power stations and the National Grid, gas distribution networks, reservoirs and water pipelines. These assets required maintenance and periodic renewal. Everyone knew this but Big Business maximises profits and minimises investment.

Sure enough when the infrastructure eventually wears out and needs major investment, guess who picks up the bill?

At first look it is quite remarkable what some governments can get away with. But that too is a special skill honed at those universities teaching politics and economics. More and more of these young graduates go straight into Westminster and become researchers, interns or assistants to a sitting MP, to learn the art of politics, and it is more a matter of expediency rather than conviction which dictates the party they join. That fits well into the Westminster pattern, but is does not provide the essential breadth of real life experience essential to good government.

The London credo is that it all has to pay its way and that means a return on private capital. That inevitably leaves the faceless taxpayer to pick up the inevitable pieces. Gamblers have an old aphorism oft quoted by Warren Buffett - "If you don't know who the sucker is, then you're it." Unlike the gambler who may just occasionally win, the taxpayer never does.

Bureaucracy

On a lighter note, no critique of the Westminster system would be complete without some reference to bureaucracy and the Yes

Minister syndrome, whereby public attention is diverted from unpopular or failing policies to trivia.

The technique is to ignore the fundamentals, and engage people's attention on energetic activities which appear to be addressing the issue, but are primarily a distraction to take the public's mind elsewhere:

> *"When you discover that you are riding a dead horse, the best strategy is to dismount."* However, in government more advanced strategies are often employed, such as:
> 1. Buying a stronger whip.
> 2. Changing riders.
> 3. Appointing a committee to study the horse.
> 4. Arranging to visit other countries to see how other cultures ride dead horses.
> 5. Lowering the standards so that dead horses can be included.
> 6. Reclassifying the dead horse as living-impaired.
> 7. Hiring outside contractors to ride the dead horse.
> 8. Harnessing several dead horses together to increase speed.
> 9. Providing additional funding and/or training to increase the dead horse's performance.
> 10. Doing a productivity study to see if lighter riders would improve the dead horse's performance.
> 11. Declaring that as the dead horse does not have to be fed, it is less costly, carries lower overhead and therefore contributes substantially more to the bottom line of the economy than do some other horses.
> 12. Rewriting the expected performance requirements for all horses, and, of course...
> 13. Promoting the dead horse to a supervisory position.

A degree of bureaucracy is undoubtedly part of all government, because there are so many departments and structures to administer that it would be impossible without 'systems'. It would seem reasonable to expect that the larger the state the greater the number of Sir Humphreys, however the reverse undoubtedly holds true, the smaller the state structure the more ridiculous the Sir Humphreys appear.

Hopefully an independent Scotland will avoid the bureaucracy trap.

The media, which is largely controlled by Big Business, is quick to tell us how business-like and efficient the Westminster model is, and to explain away this crippling public debt as public sector profligacy and the fault of the previous administration.

The truth is quite different and these observations chime with the conclusions of Chapter Five – the system of financial capitalism cannot operate without constantly escalating debt. That is why we refer to it as systemic debt.

It is the liability of the taxpayer and the asset of Big Business. It is a system supported by all the main Westminster parties. Some say it always survives its periodic crises, but is this just a periodic crisis or is this one something more? The debt mountain certainly has no historic precedent. What really matters however is how much longer it will be tolerated by the other 99%?

Employment - the Priority

It is an unforgivable crime for any society to condemn large numbers of its people, particularly its young people, to unemployment. Figures recently released show that Glasgow has the worse level of unemployment in the UK, with one third of households in the city having no-one of working age in employment.

Scotland's largest city in that appalling situation shames the whole nation, and is of course a disaster for the many people involved. Quite frankly, if this is the best the UK economy can provide, it is high time for change. We have shown that this high unemployment is entirely man-made. It is down to the failure of the government to properly manage the economy. We have also shown that a government can, and with reference to the Attlee government, has in the past solved the unemployment problem.

The way forward is for a newly independent Scotland to take a more radical and more fundamental approach to our economic future. Franklin D Roosevelt when proposing to implement the New Deal famously said *"The only thing we have to fear is fear itself"*. Those famous words are as appropriate in the run-up to the referendum as they were in 1933.

Markets – the Lessons

Much human hardship and suffering has been caused by governments which imposed a policy of free markets and non-intervention. Conversely, we have witnessed how command economies, such as that established in the Soviet Union, when it adopted the view that consumer selection was not important, and that the economy would be better served by a committee of experts, failed. That spectacular failure, in a mountain of economic waste and corruption, led to even greater hardship for ordinary people.

Adam Smith was right about the market, it can indeed perform an important role through consumer selection and prioritising production. But Marx and Keynes were also right to point out that the market cannot deal with every aspect of economic development. The economy is living and vibrant; it demands constant care and attention. That includes monitoring its dynamic cycles to ensure it performs its primary function of generating sustainable wealth across the entire community. Again, that is more readily accomplished in a smaller country, as is evident today in Europe.

Globalisation

Globalisation supports its own bureaucracy through international institutions like the World Bank, the IMF and the World Trade Organisation. These organisations are a mixture of international politics and Big Business and are the main promoters of globalisation. If that word meant the promotion of genuine fair trade principles based on fair wages and working conditions and a reasonable profit for participating enterprises, then globalisation could be a force for good. Unfortunately, the contrary is the case, and they are driven by exactly the same vested interests that dictate the policies of Westminster and Washington.

When our politicians say that in this age of globalisation the small nation has no influence, this has to be understood as self-interested propaganda. Globalisation is driven by Big Business and international banking and their image is fronted by politicians who share their credo. No small country should feel obliged or intimidated by such propaganda, and should concentrate upon arranging its affairs for the benefit of its own people first, and for the 'international community', whatever that might mean, second.

At the end of the day the futile attempts to reduce these issues to whether we are all a few hundred pounds better or worse off as a result of independence, has no substance in a world where money itself is meaningless, and is not related to physical resources. It is much more important that we feel valued within our community, rather than exist as pawns on the board of someone else's business game.

It is about trusting your government to act in the common interest, and being accountable, and knowing that if it is contemplating doing something you don't like then you can get close enough to ensure you can do something about it.

So let us make sure we insist upon proper democratic accountability, and keep a close eye on international business interests and their paid lobbyists' intent upon influencing our politicians and democratic institutions

PART TWO

A Scottish Currency

INTRODUCTION

It is October 2014, and the Scots have just voted YES to independence. You are in Holyrood and have invited the chairman of one of the big banks to advise the best banking and monetary policy for Scotland.

Odds are he would suggest retaining sterling and banking laws similar to those of the present regime. He might suggest that a Scottish Banking Commissioner be appointed to represent Scotland at the Bank of England, and to assist the Solicitor General in drafting the Scottish banking laws to a well proven pattern adopted in most developed nations – etcetera, etcetera, etcetera.

You might wish a second opinion and who better than the senior professor of economics from a prestigious Scottish University. No one could fault you for going to the top for the best advice.

Again you would be quite surprised to hear anything much different from the academic establishment. He is teaching the next generation of economic advisors in the time proven methodology that he in his turn was taught as a student. Like the chairman of the bank he is well paid and secure in his status. *"Stick to the tried and tested; we understand the business cycle and the good times are just around the corner. Please accept this complimentary copy of my latest book."*

Perhaps, however, you are something more than a career politician, with a degree in politics and economics from yet another prestigious university. Perhaps, you are in politics to try and make a difference. Perhaps, as you sit back and mull over the advice of these eminent experts there is an uncomfortable niggle in the back of your mind.

It says, *"You know these are the guys who represent the status quo, the Establishment. These are the people who guided us into where we are today. They do not want change. They are not restless entrepreneurs and they are not the discoverers of penicillin or television, or even the humble bicycle".*

This niggle just won't go away and you feel you have been given the power to make things better. You have several researchers who will do your bidding. Where do you turn, are there other avenues to explore? Where are they, and if you find them, have you the nerve to think 'outside the box'? Where would you start?

Well, that's what this book is for, and it dots every 'i' and crosses every 't' in its task of presenting the alternative.

The question is of course, are you too busy to be open minded, too preoccupied to see the wood for the trees?

So Part Two is about how we will pay for the new Scotland, and how we would finance our private and public lives. You will find the institutions we are suggesting are familiar, but they work differently. That is because they are re-designed to serve the community of Scotland and will be accountable to them. It is made possible because we are an old state making a new start with minimal baggage.

There are some new ideas, but this is more about reinstating principles and integrity into our banking and financial services. Much of this may seem innovative to an entire generation, but the process is largely informed by historic precedent. Pivotal to this is the concept of Constitutional Money which restores the origination and issue of the National Currency from the private banks to the State. It is a change, designed to rejuvenate every sector of our debt-ridden society.

Countless battles between moneylenders and the State have been recorded since the first coins were struck, and in the first chapter there is a potted history of money.

However, to illustrate the pedigree of Constitutional Money, here is a short extract from A History of Monetary Systems by Alexander del Mar, published in 1895.

In his preface he confesses –

"That which has engaged the attention without harmonising the convictions of such master minds as Aristotle, Plato, Tyco Brahe, Copernicus, Locke, Newton, Smith, Bastia, and Mill, is surely a study which none can afford to approach with rashness, nor to leave with complacency......

and some 500 pages later on Constitutional Money, del Mar writes – *...that the State or Crown should resume its ancient prerogative; the State now is identical to the Crown, for the State alone can stop the alternate melting down, shipping to and fro, and re-coinages of metal which lie at the base of monetary disturbances. The contention henceforth may be not whether the symbols of money shall be made of one metal or of two metals, but that **the State and not the money-changers shall control its issues."***

Del Mar wrote in an era of gold sovereigns and dollars, and with paper banknotes which were exchangeable for gold on demand, and when nations settled their international debts by shipping bullion around the world. We now work with fiat currencies, of which more later, but del Mar's last phrase of his last sentence is even more apposite today.

Originating the national currency in this manner as described above is pivotal – it is the loom upon which we weave our money system into the fabric of our society.

Money becomes a tool of government enabling it to manage full and gainful employment, by directing capital investment into public assets without incurring public debt. It restores openness and accountability, and provides the optimal platform for a private sector engaged in useful free enterprise rather than inflating financial bubbles.

The essence of any money system is integrity, and it matters not whether it is based on gold, a basket of commodities, or, as we advocate here, is a well managed fiat system. Integrity starts by removing its issue from private hands and placing it with the State. That integrity is further enhanced when it is taken out of the hands of the political administration and rested in the Constitution.

That alone however is not sufficient, as witnessed in 1913 in the United States, and in Chapter 6 we address this matter in some detail, with specific provisions. Even with these limitations, it is many orders of magnitude a great deal better than prevailing arrangements.

A fiat currency is the ideal money system, but it is vulnerable to manipulation because it is conceptual rather than physical. It may be likened to the money in a game of Monopoly, in that it works well provided the rules are scrupulously observed by all the players. If, however, the banker competes with the other players and abuses his trust, he will inevitably win the game. Monopoly has been nicknamed the 'Capitalist Game'. All currency systems provide a means of exchange, but only a constitutional fiat system provides the means of optimising the economy.

Once honest money enters circulation, it is the focus of an economic system full of hazards and potential corruption both by circumstance and by design of the less scrupulous.

So there must be rules to keep it honest. To consider that the responsibility of the State ends here would be like designing a perfect football and expecting the players to conduct an equally perfect football match without a referee or any further rules. In a later chapter we describe the Virtuous Circle – the main financial organs and institutions of state, and their relationship to the private sector, thus guarding against domestic and foreign predation.

The strategy of the Virtuous Circle defends the freedom of the individual and the integrity of the currency from those external forces which experience has shown to be malignant. From this will flow options which make financially possible that which is also socially desirable and physically possible, not least full employment, sustainable pensions and public services.

It is a strategy designed to defend democracy against the worst excesses of financial capitalism – just as we maintain our military forces to defend against internal or external attack or invasion.

CHAPTER 8

History of Public Debt

This financial crisis is very much about huge public debt, which seems to have crept up upon us almost unnoticed. Oh yes, we have all heard about the National Debt and how it took a jump when we had to finance two world wars, and some of us even understood how peacetime governments of all stripes frequently miscalculated the national budget and had to borrow to make up the shortfall. But how on earth did this get so out of hand – not just for the UK but for so many countries including the mighty United States?

To answer that you will be glad to hear that this chapter is more about debt than history, although knowing how we got here is the first step to finding our way out. We shall discover how in more recent times nations managed to build up the monumental burdens of debt which today govern our lives and cripple our economies.

You may have heard that the first coins were invented by the King of Lydia in the 6th Century BC. In fact there is evidence to suggest that Darius brought back silver coins from his earlier expedition down the River Indus in modern day Pakistan.

Be that as it may, ever since alchemists tried to turn base metal into gold, mankind has tried to make money out of nothing – or at least with as little hard work as possible.

We shall however confine ourselves to the relatively recent past when credit ceased to mean waiting a month to get your bill paid and started to be used as money.

In England, this is where the goldsmiths come in.

In the mid 17th Century anyone having gold (or silver), could deposit it with a Goldsmith who would keep it safe in his vault. In return, the goldsmith would give the depositor a note or notes which 'promised to pay the bearer' the sum of money deposited. These notes could be returned to the goldsmith at any time, to get the pieces of precious metal back.

Of course, the new notes were far more convenient to carry about than the heavy coins, far safer too. Soon people were happy to use the pieces of paper that represented the precious metal coins as if they were those very same bits of shiny metal. Nothing wrong with that, coins as a means of exchange, paper as a means of exchange, it's in the vault – no problem.

However, at some point the goldsmiths realised that although people were depositing their money with them, at any one time only a fraction of the promissory notes would be returned. Some worked out that only 10% were being returned. This led to a very neat scam.

If the goldsmiths only had to return 10% of the gold that was deposited with them, then they could lend the rest of the gold to other people for a rate of interest.

Even better, they could lend out promissory notes, as the notes were regarded to be as good as the precious metal coins, literally 'as good as gold'. All they had to do is keep 10% of the value of the issued notes as gold or silver in the vault, just in case someone wanted to cash them in. Of course you can't expect to borrow money, just because you ask. The goldsmiths would require something to be secured against the loan, something of value, like your house.

So, if a goldsmith had say, £1,000 worth of coins in the vault and this could equal 10% of the money he loaned out, allowing for the original promissory notes given to the depositors, the goldsmith could lend out another £9,000 worth of notes.

In other words the goldsmiths discovered that they could obtain nine times the amount of money (and interest) on coins that other people had deposited in the vault. Money that wasn't even theirs!

This was a risk, but as long as everybody didn't ask for the coins back at the same time, everything was okay. So keep it secret, okay?

Now the problem lies here, because people needed money and so systemic debt came into existence – debt contractually owed to a private party, the goldsmith, issued against money which did not exist. It was a new kind of alchemy but it was also fraud.

The most successful crimes are those no one knows about. They tend to be small fry and non-violent. Fraud is a good crime in this respect, because even if is discovered it is notoriously difficult to prove in court, and although it starts out small it has unlimited potential.

The perfect fraud however is ambitious, and requires the selection of a 'mark' holding political power, and who can become unwittingly embroiled. This ploy ensures that if the scheme misfires it will be covered up, and if it succeeds it can become institutionalised into the structure of political power. It thus perpetuates itself to the benefit of all its heirs and successors. In short it becomes institutionalised and legitimate under the laws of the land.

This is summarised in a short verse describing the '*Enclosures in England*' during the 17th century. Much common land was just 'stolen' from the community by aristocrats and the practice was upheld by the courts - which were run by the same aristocrats.

The law doth punish man or woman

That steals the goose from off the common,

But lets the greater felon loose

That steals the common from the goose

Anonymous 17th Century

This old adage chimes with the founding of the Bank of England in 1694. The bank was the idea of a crafty Scotsman called William Paterson.

The King needed £1.2 million to pay the army and our Willie came up with the original pyramid deal – I'll raise £1.2 million in gold for you if you give me the right to print £1.2 million in paper banknotes. The King agreed and overnight £1.2 million became £2.4 million. Paterson did not own the gold but like the goldsmiths, collected interest on the banknotes when he loaned them to his customers.

Thus banking as we know it today became enshrined by parliament two years later, disguised as The Tonnage Act – ostensibly dealing with tariffs and taxes with the establishment of the bank as a subsidiary issue.

Then, as now, most politicians either did not understand what they were approving, or alternatively considered it to be in their best interests. In fairness we must also keep in mind that in those days this was not a democratically elected legislature, but a body of the privileged elected by the privileged and for the benefit of the privileged.

With the passage of time banking prospered, and for almost three hundred years was conducted relatively responsibly by succeeding Acts of Parliament which kept its worst excesses within bounds.

Banks went bust occasionally, but were never too big to fail. The loans they made were also mainly commercial, and as private house ownership became progressively more common with the rise of the middle classes in the mid nineteenth century, so Building Societies were established, which up until their demise in the 1980's provided virtually all of the loans required for house purchases – some 75% of all loans in the UK. The banks were simply not involved in home mortgages. *(See Appendix 1)*.

Let us return however, to the beginning of debt-money in 1695. William of Orange, (he was King at the time), had established the Bank of England so that he could borrow money in order to fight the French. But going to war doesn't usually result in a financial profit, there are too many outgoings; weapons, soldiers, food, uniforms, boats etc.

William didn't worry about all that, instead he created the national debt and left the taxpayers to pay the interest.

Of course the bank is never really concerned about repayment of the principal – it was created from nothing in the first place, and as long as the taxpayer keeps forking out the interest, then they will not complain. The taxpayer, who had no say in the matter in any case, will not repay the principal and so it keeps rolling over – it is systemic debt, and it is simple maths to conclude that when the interest becomes unsustainable, the system must collapse.

Paying back a debt with interest however, did concern Abraham Lincoln. When Abraham needed money to fund the American Civil War, he went to the banks and said something like, "I need some money and lots of it. I'm going to war."

The banks in return said something like, "That's great. We can loan you all the money you need, but war is a risky business, we'll have to charge you far more than our usual rate of interest".

Abe probably said, "That's outrageous", and stormed off. So instead of borrowing money from the banks he decided to create it himself. He got the US government to issue 'Greenbacks', and bought all the items he needed for the war with them. Everyone had confidence in the money that President Lincoln had issued, so everyone was happy to buy and sell with the new notes.

This new money wasn't backed by gold or silver; it was backed by something better than that - the President's word, or the government, or the taxpayer. It was worth what it said it was worth on the note. The new money worked just like the bankers money. There was one big difference though, when the war finished and Lincoln had won, the USA didn't have to pay back a huge loan, and they certainly didn't have to pay any interest.

This gave Lincoln an idea. If I can create money to go to war, just think of all the other things I could do. I could issue some money to build Government constructions to make sure our people were properly trained, healthy and well educated. A pension when they retire possibly.

But before Lincoln could do any of this he was assassinated. Not that Lincoln's assassination had anything to do with his new money strategy, but that was the end of that idea.

In summary, it has always been the duty of a State to provide a National Currency. That currency was fed into circulation through the banking system entirely free of public debt. It became private debt when the banks loaned it out. Paterson's £1.2 million of paper money was convertible into gold upon demand when presented to the bank. That principle kept the lid on credit creation until the early 1970's when the final gold link to the U.S. dollar was severed.

The bankers understood this, but the politicians and regulators did not. The consequences are plain to see, and if this irrational process is ever to return to public accountability then the origination of national currencies must be limited by the Constitution.

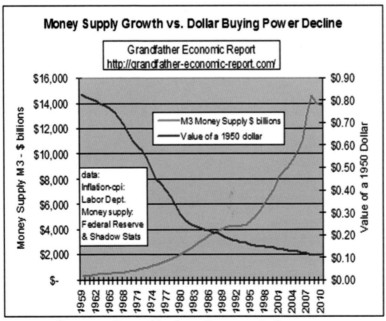

Source: _Grandfather Economic Report_

CHAPTER 9

The Imperative of Reform

Why reform is essential. The desperate need to reform western money and currency systems is apparent but political initiatives, let alone agreement on how, is totally absent - ending the ill conceived era of privately issued money - the place of gold and the option of a true fiat currency and how it can be optimised and directed to stimulate social progress. Refocusing from banking as just another business and on to the needs of the wider society and how it can be done – a taste of the theme of this whole work

Part One concluded with a vision of what many will perceive as a pipe dream for Scotland – a well adjusted, socially cohesive society, fully employed within a prosperous domestic economy – independent, but internationally highly regarded.

We may or may not achieve this, but unless we know where we are headed, and how we can finance the journey, then we will remain trapped in someone else's land, directed by a government we did not elect, and directed towards objectives in which we do not share a common purpose.

There are voices in the electoral wilderness, voices saying don't forget how we got into this interminable depression; don't forget RBS and HBoS; don't forget Greece and Ireland and Portugal; don't forget the bankers' bonuses and don't forget that printing money causes inflation, unemployment and a stagnant economy.

Don't forget negative equity on your house and the huge rewards for tax dodgers and financial engineers, nor the lack of overdrafts for small business, nor the millions squandered on obsequious consultants and useless job creation initiatives

Keep in mind the dogma of controlling inflation with interest rates, which have destroyed your pensions and any incentive to save, and don't forget that we need our jobs if we are to pay off the money lenders and be allowed to borrow even more.

Finally and most of all, remember the financial experts who advised the governors of this asylum who created this chaos, are the same financial advisors who tell us we can't really afford independence in the first place. Could we do better? How can it be done?

Certainly it is an agenda inconceivable within the Westminster parliament and unaffordable in terms of the financial constraints imposed by the City of London. The prospect can be explored only within a very different political and financial framework, and here in Part Two, it is my job to describe the means by which we can make it financially possible.

Like it or not, we live in a world dominated by money. Listen to any radio or TV current affairs programme and count the times you hear the words money, debt, bank, credit, borrowing, interest, cost, lending, and afford. That is because virtually every activity is measured in monetary terms. We have been brainwashed into believing that community progress is rationed by affordability rather than what is achievable, socially desirable and personally fulfilling.

Money is no longer there to facilitate our ambitions, it has become an end in itself – the dominant end.

Ours is a world controlled by moneylenders – big business money lending. It is a culture born of gold and silver, which should have withered when we all adopted fiat currencies, but as always the moneylenders have survived and prospered.

This may be the choice of some individuals, but it can't be acceptable within the management of a progressive community. In a democracy the voters elect representatives to conduct their affairs in the interests of the whole community, and not in accordance with rules set by banking corporations, particularly those dependent upon charters granted and guaranteed by their host community.

We have witnessed a succession of world leaders meeting to resolve this latest and greatest financial disaster. Individual leaders and their governments have responded to calls for reform of the banks, and we have seen nothing more than anodyne official inquiries and cosmetic tinkering in a pathetic cover-up for actually doing anything. It has become apparent that the banking system is now fully integrated into the political establishment and any serious attempt at reform would risk bringing down the whole house of cards. So why should an independent Scotland fare any better?

The main advantage of having a new independent Scotland is because it can start from scratch, without all the trappings of corruption and vested interest accumulated over hundreds of years of political and financial manipulation. It has no baggage, no skeletons in cupboards; it can be done, given the will.

But can Scots shed the mind-set, centuries of feeling subservient to those who control the money system, the money we must all borrow and which we are so familiar with?

It must be recognised that our relationship with money is a factor which weighs heavily upon our minds and into our political thinking, so we need to think clearly about it.

We need to question not only the justice, but the logic of supporting a system of government which is subordinate to moneylenders, because that ensures a society governed by debt rather than enterprise and progress. This book is about re-assessing values and making the best use of our lives and times.

The Scots can be a thrawn bunch of folk, and perhaps a third of them are pledged to vote for Independence in the upcoming Referendum of September 2014. Encouraged to believe that they might also achieve financial independence into the bargain they might just bring that third up to over 50%. That however means using your vote to support candidates you believe can share this vision of something new and different, and who also possess the nerve and drive to throw out the moneylenders and grasp the financial bull by the horns.

Given that the Scots say YES in 2014, the top priority of the first administration is to consider the new nation's Banking System and Monetary Policy. Getting that right will open many doors; stick with sterling, and the Bank of England, and nothing will change but the name above the door.

Many years ago government was gullible enough to allow private banks to issue some of the nation's money. Today, amidst the ruins of an economy destroyed by bankers' greed, government is not only permitting them to rebuild to the same pattern as before, but we taxpayers are being obliged to re-finance them. This is either crass stupidity or blatant corruption but either way it is their monetary policy – and our burden.

Monetary policy is made wilfully and complicated by those who benefit from it. To those ordinary citizens who say they do not understand it, and do not wish to understand it, then it is their choice to opt out – but it is not the right of any MP, MSP, Public Servant or Trade Union Official, because they accept a salary and expenses for protecting the public interest.

Monetary policy presently serves the rich and powerful and it will stay that way until the rest of us take time to read the boring small print and demand reform. Let no one believe that monetary policy is not important. Its tentacles reach into every crevice of society.

An element of instability is inherent in all economies, but unemployment should be regarded as a criminal offence on the part of any government which condones it.

Unemployment is a waste of resources yes, but more importantly it destroys people's self respect and quality of life. It is the core of a dysfunctional society. The dogma that 'we' cannot afford to put the unemployed to work on creating useful public assets is a further example of brainwashing by the elite

Monetary policy affects every one of us intimately. It dictates how we interact with each other, and with the economy. We should discourage measuring literally every value in terms of money, and encourage a resurgence of community and national character. This should be the hot topic of the 'National Conversation'; getting it right should be up there in the top three reasons why we need Independence – and unlike oil revenues, its dividends will last indefinitely.

The wealth of nations is not measured in how many money tokens they can print, it is not even measured in the statistics of GDP – it is to be found in how we value the wellbeing of our society.

With these thoughts in mind, let us start by asking – what makes an ideal money system?

It is first and foremost 'Integrity'. A state monopoly under the Constitution; it is issued without the debt which has destroyed the present system. It is isolated from influence by the incumbent administration, service to the community is its primary objective. All new money issued under the Constitution must be matched to creating new community assets (see Chapter 13), and function as a tool of community economic management.

The system must also be proof against counterfeit & fraud at issue, and thereafter by foreigners beyond legal scrutiny. When money is deposited with an authorised bank it must remain the property of the depositor. There should be a preferred status for mutually owned banks having genuine member representation in the boardroom.

We need legislation to encourage pension & insurance funds to invest in banks to fund the means of exchange. We should prohibit governments making long term borrowing with no intention to repay the principal, as this is essential to capping public debt. We must give freedom to governments to regulate terms of credit to match economic objectives, rather than private profit incentive. These represent broad principles and are not exclusive. Greater detail is provided in subsequent pages.

Up until 1950 the UK money system has generally been split between the State, the building societies, and the private banks. In 1951 the State still produced half the money in circulation by way of cash and notes. This was debt free money which was sent to the banks as required to meet the public demand for cash. It was issued debt free by the Central Bank (Bank of England), on authority of the Treasury, and the amount was credited to the government's account by the receiving bank. This is known as 'seigniorage', and when the government drew a cheque on this account it was free of debt.

Gradually, with the advent of universal checking accounts, consumer and electronic bank credit, the demand for cash reduced progressively until, in 2001, it amounted to only 3% of circulating money – just three pence in every pound. Seigniorage was a significant element of debt free finance for government, now virtually lost.

The building societies figured prominently in personal finances until their absorption into the banking system post 1986. Prior to that time they provided some 75% of all private debt in the UK, and they financed virtually 100% of private house mortgages – all fully funded by their saving members. On average it took seven savers to fund a mortgage. (*See Appendix. 1*).

A further anomaly is that private banks also grant credit to governments by purchasing their official bonds or securities. These normally carry a low interest coupon because governments are not expected to default on these – not in terms of repayment, because they were never expected to repay them, but in terms of interest payments. If however, a government consistently fails to balance its budget then the rating agencies can downgrade the status of this debt which usually means an increase in the rate of interest paid.

Default has occurred in the past, not because the principal has not been repaid, but because the burden of interest becomes so great as to be unsustainable. That can lead to actual default when the bank has to admit that the loan has become a bad debt and is obliged to write it off and charge the loss against its own capital and reserves. This is what we see in the Eurozone – a threat to bring down the affected banks unless rescued by the ultimate lender of last resort – nominally the European Central Bank, but in fact the taxpayer. That poses the question – who runs the country, the government or the banks?

For all these reasons and perhaps more, the rate of growth of public debt has reached levels unsupportable by further taxation, but more importantly it is systemic debt – debt generated by a malignant system bent upon destroying its host. That is now so obvious that surely it can no longer be ignored.

There has also been considerable speculation about the return of gold, which used to provide the backing to most currencies, and this has led to speculation that a return to some form of gold standard for currencies would resolve this instability. The price of gold has also kept pace with inflation over the long term and is seen by many investors as a safe haven for savings. A significant increase in demand for gold has also caused concern within the banking system as this could signal the return of some control over their freedom to manipulate currencies and bank credit creation.

The power of the banking interests is being tested at the time of writing as the big bullion banks effectively control the price of gold through the daily 'fix' of gold prices in the bullion market. So far they have succeeded in introducing significant instability into the official gold prices in their efforts to confront this threat.

Further instability is caused by the introduction of 'paper gold' in the form of 'Exchange Tradable Funds', which are promises to buy or sell gold at some future date. There are presently some 100 times as many of these promises in circulation as there is physical gold in the world. (*See Chapter 10 and Appendix 4*).

No national currencies are presently linked to gold reserves – although unofficially the Swiss Franc approaches this with perhaps 20% of its value matched to official gold holdings.

A totally reconstituted IMF might call upon its 187 member states to maintain a minimum deposit with it, of say 20% of the value of their issued currency in gold, with an automatic sanction of devaluation upon default. There is certainly sufficient gold in the world to facilitate this, and such an agreement has much to commend it.

This has connotations with the Bancor system devised by John Maynard Keynes - an excellent means of managing the balance of payments between nations, but rejected by Dexter White of the USA at Bretton Woods in 1945. However, the IMF, based in Washington DC is very much an instrument of White House political and financial policy and therefore unlikely to change its character in the foreseeable future.

A fixed link to gold would automatically spell the end of unlimited privately issued bank credit, but would also acknowledge our inability to manage our means of exchange on any intellectual basis. Moreover, it would fall far short of reintroducing constitutional money as proposed here, because apart from providing a stable means of exchange, a sovereign fiat currency is an invaluable tool for any government pledged to a fairer and sustainable society.

Fiat means faith in a paper currency of no intrinsic value and having no link to precious metals or any commodity. Its integrity is a reflection of the integrity of the government which issues it and the strength of its economy.

The fiat system is in common use throughout the world, but it has been distorted beyond recognition by gross abuse. Any national currency is 'sovereign' in that it is authorized and issued exclusively by the state as exemplified by cash and notes which are sent in bulk to the banks for distribution.

The abuse occurs when banks issue money above and beyond this sovereign issue in the form of credit, assuming that the bank's credit will enjoy the same authority of the State and the guarantee of the taxpayer. That is a form of counterfeit legalized by custom. It could not occur if all money was still in the form of cash but has become accepted with its gradual replacement by virtually unregulated credit.

The widespread use of electronic credit has enabled the private banks to literally take over the administration of the world's main currencies, and yet they still remain guaranteed by the citizens.

The banks on the other hand, like all other corporations, are accountable to their boards and shareholders to maximize their profits and have no contractual or moral obligation to the citizen. The money system no longer belongs to the community but to a monopoly of private corporations called banks and the consequences are plain to see. Democratically elected governments are now little more than customers beholden to their banks' computers.

The low cost and convenience of credit can be fully retained whilst returning sovereignty. That is not the problem. It is that the banks are now so powerful they are holding the State to ransom – they meet any proposal for serious reform with the threat of paralyzing the entire payments system – an event which no politician dare contemplate.

This chapter opened with a call upon our first independent government to review our banking system. It has the unique opportunity to do so without the baggage of the present UK banking hegemony. That translates into a simple statement, that the origination and issue of new money, whether as credit or cash, is the sole prerogative of the State and that would make it a true sovereign currency.

That means that neither a bank, nor any other private agency, may create cash or issue credit as Principals, but must act as Intermediaries between the State and its citizens.

That in turn means that notional money created by foreign banks cannot be permitted to 'compete' with the state by issuing credit within its borders, and the only way to stop that is by declaring that only the national currency shall be legal tender. That would clearly be impossible if sterling, or any other currency was free to circulate as a means of payment.

This is the fundamental change of attitude towards money and banking advocated in the following pages. It makes full and gainful employment achievable; it offers a realistic system of funding public services and it means the stability of an independent currency serving the citizen rather than the bankers.

That opens doors presently closed to the people of the UK.

CHAPTER 10

Financial Markets

Financial Markets are the engines which manufacture obscene profits and bonuses from the notional credit provided by interbank lending. How this generates instability on an international scale and how it would wither in the wake of banking reform.

Financial markets are where investment bankers ply their trade. They are where bankers' bonuses come from, and where financial crises are hatched. They are sometimes referred to as casinos but they are not. If you bet at a casino you know the chances are the house will win, and you will lose. You also know that if you gamble and can't afford to lose, or use someone else's money then you are on a slippery slope. You know also that if you conspired to cheat, or failed to settle your losses, then at best you would end up in court, or at worst, be found much the worse for wear down some sleazy back alley. Gambling is a personal choice with personal outcomes which do not impact upon society as a whole. None of these considerations apply in financial markets.

Unlike the glitzy casinos of Las Vegas or the Riviera, financial markets are hidden away from the public eye. Even the term 'market' is designed to confuse because nothing tangible is bought or sold in these halls of electronic smoke and mirrors. They are devices of the aptly named Shadow Banking System. That is the modern day term for alchemy - the philosopher's stone which could be turned into gold.

It is an illusion of course just as it always has been, but it is much easier to turn electronic bank credit into private profit, than to turn stone or base metal into gold. As with all illusions it is obscured by a good story and that story is entitled Shadow Banking.

No news programme from the BBC would be complete without a report from the 'markets'. The inference being that they are essential elements of contemporary economics and shape our destinies. They are portrayed as reacting to external and political forces but closer examination reveals this volatility is generated internally by the markets themselves, in anticipating their own response, a process usually initiated by the financial media, which is of course a major contributor to the illusion.

These markets have no 'product' other than to destabilise the financial system, because without predictable volatility there would be little profit incentive for the participants.

Make no mistake, these activities are the hatcheries of financial chaos, and they operate on the edge of the law.

Those at the top of this 'profession' are rich and powerful; they carry significant political and media influence; they are represented in the high offices of state, and measure success in terms of how much money they can accumulate. They despise lesser mortals and their eyes are tight shut to the misery and despair they cause. They justify financial markets as essential to free enterprise and competition and scorn state intervention as communist dogma.

What they do is immoral and irrational; but they do not believe it is unsustainable any more than any other parasite has qualms about killing its host, because each generation produces an endless supply of victims. They are the modern day 'parcel of rogues' - the 0.1% - the Financial Capitalists.

If they are to be expunged then we need to expose the illusion.

Financial markets deal in paper promises to buy or sell a financial asset, which is in itself just another promise. If you or I decided to participate in these games we would require to 'take a position', which means finding a broker and putting a very large stake up front. It would be a pure gamble because we are not part of the inner circle. The inner circle is actually a hierarchy of players, but they do not gamble, they follow the lead of the top guns, and as a rule the top guns do not lose, because they have access to an unlimited supply of other people's money.

The top guns are the big banks, which either directly or through an intermediary 'take a huge position' on whatever commodity or derivative they target. They use the virtually unlimited credit to which they have access, and buy and sell promises on the margin.

These could involve almost anything, from oil to interest rates, pork bellies to orange juice or foreign currencies – all and anything where prices move. Their trades are so large as to influence market prices and with this inside information they can 'rig' the market.

Further down the hierarchy there are traders who understand what is happening, and join the food chain at lower levels. The lower down the chain the riskier it becomes, and sometimes real money is lost – but not often.

A plethora of such activities constitute the bulk of financial markets. The market traders have no intention of taking physical delivery of any of the items they deal in – they are concerned only with price movements up or down. There are paper promises called derivatives being traded today which amount to some twenty times the world's GDP.

In the gold market there are 100 times as many promises to buy gold as exist in physical terms. It becomes clear that these are not market places where real goods and services are traded – they are devices having no function other than to enrich the key participants. The fact that in the course of this so called trading the prices of virtually everything we buy and sell is 'rigged', is of no consequence to these people, and their victims are virtually everyone else who participates in the economy of the real world. This whole pyramid is financed with bank credit emitted from the fractional reserve banking system and guaranteed by ordinary taxpayers.

In 2012 the LIBOR (London Inter-Bank Official Rate) scandal surfaced. This is the rate of interest at which the big banks lend to one another. It was exposed as a criminal fraud, and in the US was an indictable offence, although of course no one has gone to prison.

The rate was fixed by the banker's trade association the British Bankers Association, and traders say the practice goes back decades. This is just one of the many ways financial markets are fixed so as to enrich the principle operators, and the absence of meaningful prosecution confirms the power of these people in high places.

The gold price scam of early 2013 illustrates the complicity of our ostensibly 'democratic institutions' – our Central Banks:

* Central banks all over the world hold gold bullion.

* They 'lease' large quantities of this gold to one of half a dozen international bullion mega banks, for a nominal rate of less than 1%. The gold does not normally physically leave the vault

* The banks sell the gold into the market in such quantities as to control the 'natural' price.

* They invest the proceeds in government bonds paying 5%. This supports the value of fiat currencies against the natural rise in gold prices to reflect inflation.

* The bullion banks control the gold price because they have a monopoly over virtually unlimited amounts of this 'paper' gold which they can dump onto the market to depress the official price.

* As long as the Central Banks do not demand the termination of the lease contract, the paper gold continues to generate huge profits for the megabanks.

* The problem is that millions of individuals, and Asian governments, are buying all the physical gold they can and taking actual delivery of it. So paper gold is becoming a 'claim' on a non-existent commodity.

* Most of the gold leased out is still in the vaults of the central banks. If they asked for the leased gold to be returned the price of gold would rocket and the chances are the bullion banks would go bust, thus triggering another financial crisis.

- No central bank wants another financial crisis so the contracts keep rolling over.

Chapter 8 described the perfect fraud as being 'ambitious', and requires the selection of a 'mark' holding political power and who can become unwittingly embroiled. This ploy ensures that if the scheme misfires it will be covered up and if it succeeds it can become institutionalised into the structure of political power. It thus perpetuates itself to the benefit of all its heirs and successors.

In short it becomes institutionalised and legitimate under the 'laws of the land'. That referred to the Tonnage Act which established the Bank of England. Nothing has changed but the name of the game. If you would like a flavour of how this particular illusion is conducted, please see *Appendix 3*.

If, instead of the market analysts and neo liberal economists, an engineer or a scientist started looking into these markets they might conclude that these are not markets at all. They are pseudo criminal organisations thinly disguised as ordinary markets. The enquiring mind would then require an explanation of why such activities, having worldwide repercussions, should escape the attention of legislators and lawmakers, and here they would move from the smoke and mirrors into the world of politics and human frailty.

These 'markets' might be summarised thus:

- They are not markets, as no tangible goods or services are exchanged or delivered.

- They are intentionally volatile and this translates into instability in the physical economy

- They are criminal because they use other peoples credit without their consent

- They could not exist without the complicity of the Fractional Reserve Banking System.

Honest money is earned by ordinary people who engage in the

exchange of goods and services among one another, and they pay taxes to support the public services provided by government. That same government should be the sole source of the national currency which, as everyone knows, is guaranteed by the taxpayer, and it is issued to facilitate useful and productive activity among the population.

Dishonest money is not issued by the State but by the banks in the form of credit. Some of that credit is honest because banks lend out money deposited with them by their customers, but that is just a very small fraction of what they lend. That is why it is called the Fractional Reserve System and well over 95% of all money is debt owed to the banks, as explained in the following chapter. (*See Appendix 2*).

Genuine financial services suffer as a result of these mutations, and it is important to distinguish between these terms. Financial markets are not markets where you would shop for a reliable insurance policy for your house or car, nor an annuity, a mortgage, a life or endowment policy, or just a safe place to earn a fair return on your savings.

Indeed these are the very financial services which have been undermined and devalued by this murky world of global financial markets and the smoke and mirrors of shadow banking. Moreover, they also propel elected governments into some very odd decisions.

The crisis continues because first, politicians listen only to the establishment of experts who have a vested interest in the present banking, financial and academic institutions. Academics, principally down to their dislike of change, or any new order which challenges the accepted doctrine, tend to support the status quo. Secondly, politicians will, by their nature, always kick the can down the road in the hope that someone else will pick it up.

If the law was changed to outlaw fractional reserve banking within the sovereign border, the endless supply of credit to these bubbles would dry up, and they would wither and die. This is asking a lot of politicians in the UK, with the City of London at its political centre, but for a new Sovereign State starting from scratch, perfectly achievable.

The Role of the Rating Agencies

There are three principle private agencies which evaluate securities and financial assets, and grade them as to risk, return and reliability. They are included here as their assessments plays an important part in establishing financial market values, but also to explain why our democratic governments become pawns in this game of financial chess.

There is a specialised market in government bonds – the bonds issued by virtually all governments when they borrow money from banks, some of which are then sold on to pension funds and insurance companies. Bond traders buy and sell these in normal trading, and like all other financial assets the prices fluctuate. These changes are responsive to the periodic assessments of rating agencies, the prices rising or falling according to the agencies' view of the credit worthiness of the issuing government.

As with all such markets the traders speculate in anticipation of these announcements, and if a particular government is perceived to be financially vulnerable – perhaps in potential deficit on its domestic budget or balance of payments, that will affect the valuations. As valuations rise or fall so the real interest rate moves up or down and this will affect the rate a government must pay on its borrowings. This is the interest on what is now a monumental national debt.

In the UK, and in the Eurozone, the economy is stifled by this burden. In Portugal, Ireland, Italy and Spain the economy is in tatters and in Greece it is non-existent – on the verge of collapse. Governments are actually being run by what are termed technocrats – a polite name for administrators appointed by the banks and approved by the IMF – and you don't need a lot of imagination to guess where that is headed.

So at last – the punch line – who is all this debt owed to? We know we pay the interest to the banks, but where did they get all the money they have so kindly loaned to their government customers?

The answer is simple, yet another illusion called the Fractional Reserve Banking System. The bulk of this debt is systemic – a stroke of a pen, another promise of money, not real money like cash issued by the state, or earned in your pay packet, just alchemy.

The truth is that all this debt could be written off and no one would suffer – even the big banks which lie at the heart of this gigantic scam would survive with slimmer balance sheets. That it is a scam is evidenced by the taxpayer bail-outs, and the illusion of the fractional reserve banking system to be uncovered in the next chapter.

CHAPTER 11

Fractional Reserve Banking

Fractional Reserve Banking, what is it? The remarkable magic of their balance sheets - The relationship of systemic debt to public debt - The anomaly of leveraging a fiat currency. Full Reserve Banking and Building Societies - Sovereign money.

History tells us that no one ever sat down at a desk or drawing board to invent fractional reserve banking, it sort of just happened as previously described when the goldsmiths started issuing more IOUs or promises of money than they held in their vaults. Yet this is still the basis of the banking system we use worldwide today, except of course there is no link to gold left in the arrangement. So why is it called fractional reserve if there is no reserve? Nowadays the reserve refers to the funds of the shareholders who own the bank

At the end of this book you will find the Appendices, which include a section of 'Frequently Asked Questions' on this subject, but one which seems particularly fitting at this time of financial crisis is – '*Why, when it is even more obvious that it is the banking system which is the root of all our problems, is no one seriously considering other ways of conducting the banking business?*'

The answer is that having got their feet under the banking table all those years ago, the bankers bought, both physically and metaphorically political power. Then, as now, if you control the politicians you retain a licence to print money. Only a wider public appreciation of this distasteful fact and of how the fractional reserve system perpetuates itself can hope to bring reform.

There is no shortage of academic, intellectual or business

opinion supporting this view. Over many years monetary experts have endorsed a return to Full Reserve Banking, including Professor Irving Fisher, Yale University; Milton Friedman, Chicago School; Murray Rothbard, Austrian School; Professor Steve Keen, University of Sydney; Professor James Tobin, Yale University; Professor John Kay, London Business School; Sir Mervin King, former governor Bank of England; New Economics Foundation; Positive Money, and many more.

Recently, in a paper reviewing the Euro crisis, Thomas Mayer called for a return to 100% banking reserves as an essential first step if the Euro was to survive. Thomas Mayer is Senior Fellow at the Centre for Financial Studies at Goethe University Frankfurt, and Senior Advisor to Deutsche Bank. Several of these names are Nobel Prize winners in economics, but the subject seldom surfaces in the establishment media.

The term 100% or 'full reserve' is commonly used as a generic term to describe several alternatives to the fractional reserve system. In this book we are advocating the Constitutional or Sovereign Money System covered in significant technical detail by Professor Joseph Huber, (Chair of Economic and Environmental Sociology, Martin-Luther-University, Halle, Germany).

Full reserve is also of course the spirit of the 1844 Bank Charter Act that prohibited commercial banks from printing paper notes (£1, £5, £10 and so on). The anomaly is of course that every day banks grant credit which is immediately exchangeable for notes from the ATM at the door. So how do banks get around this?

Let us imagine a group of people wished to start a fractional reserve bank before the crises, say thirty years ago.

This would be a limited company, where the liabilities are limited to the amount of their share capital. First they need to be approved by exiting bankers as being 'suitable', and that means they have experience in the banking business, and are qualified to be members of the British Bankers Association.

They would then be required to raise about £5 million in capital, partly in shares, and partly in securities, to lodge with the Bank of England. The business can then be started by opening customer accounts and making loans. As a new bank they might have to start by limiting these to say £50 million – and that represents a 10% reserve.

Now as a little light relief, imagine this process with another group of people who decided to open a building society. This is what is known as a 'Mutual', because its liabilities are limited to the amount of members' savings invested. They too open their doors offering mortgages to their borrowing members and as they must be a 100% reserve lender, they need to attract £50m of savings in order to lend £50m in mortgages. That is easier to understand because it is what happens when you or I lend £100 to a friend and we expect to go without the use of that money until it is repaid. (*See Appendix 2*)

That is not what happens at your bank because no one goes without when a fractional reserve bank lends money – or more accurately, grants credit. This alchemy is accommodated by a unique but legal accountancy technique.

On the balance sheet of the bank your loan appears both as an asset and a liability; the asset is your obligation to repay the loan, and the liability is the risk of you defaulting. Try that on your next accounts and the auditor will refuse to sign them off. From there it is a short step to a fraud charge and a spell in the pokey. It is pure money creation from nothing. Mark you, if you are one of the megabanks your auditor probably charges you more fees for consultancy than for auditing, but that's another can of worms.

Having made this legal, governments have fought a losing battle to keep this system credible, by regulation and Acts of Parliament – a bit like bailing out a leaky boat rather than fixing the leak, and when the Thatcher government deregulated the banks, the leak became a terminal event, mainly because the banks started lending huge sums to one another.

Pre-Thatcher regulations had always precluded banks creating money for themselves – they were allowed to do so only as loans at interest to their customers. After the Big Bang they got around this by lending to one another, and overnight virtually unlimited credit became available to them, although of course it would need to be paid back eventually.

The fractional reserve was originally the gold remaining in the vault; then it became the amount of the shareholders' capital, but both relate to the modern term 'leverage' – the use of a small amount of money to 'magic' up a multiple, which in the more shaky enterprises of the shadow banking world were as high as 60:1 but more usually 33:1. The world average for the mega-banks is 26:1. This means that a loss of just 4% of outstanding loans would bring down the whole house of cards. A helpful diagram in the *Appendices* illustrates this well.

Whatever logic drives acceptance of leveraging, it had some connection to something physical. But since 1971 when the US dollar ceased its tenuous connection to gold, it relates to fiat currencies of no intrinsic value. It is a voucher, a paper promise to pay legal tender by the government which issues it, and it is guaranteed by the taxpayer.

That poses the obvious question - why would a government hand the privilege of leverage to private bankers to create debt, when the state could create it debt free at virtually no cost and send it to the banks for distribution under the normal banking restraints of responsibility and moral hazard?

Another Nobel laureate, Professor J.M. Buchanan of James Mason University, asks the same question but in the language of the academic.

"These characteristics (of a fiat currency) offer the explanatory basis for monetary crises, including that of 2008–9 as well as the Great Depression in the 20th century. The ultimate villain is the leveraging of monetary accounts, which allows for the transmission of initial shocks over many sectors of the inclusive economy.

Recognition of this elementary but crucial difference between commodity-based and fiat (paper) money has profound implications for institutional-constitutional design and operation. Since, under a fiat system, there is no efficiency logic for economizing on money, as such, there is no justification for traditional banking that allows for the generation of multiple account values from fractional reserve bases. The central logic of leverage banking, of any sort, is absent under the operation of a pure fiat money system. It follows that there is no economic reason why any money system, in an idealized setting, would allow for leverage at any level. No holder of a unit of money, as an entry in a balance sheet, should be authorized to lend more than the face value of this unit, quite independent of probabilistically determined expectations concerning potential redemptions."

So there you are, however you describe it this is the illogicality at the core of the present systemic debt mountain the size of which was foreseeable to any fifth former with a calculator. At the historic average interest rate of five per cent the outstanding debt doubles ever fifteen years – that is a salutary, but mathematical certainty, well beloved of moneylenders, but too often not appreciated by borrowers, and that includes governments.

The final shove may come from the financial markets themselves. The privately owned rating agencies dispense judgement on government debt by applying assessments to their bonds. As these ratings drop from the top Triple A, so the interest rate rises. As the numbers stand, it cannot be long before this impacts sterling – aggravated not just by the ongoing domestic shortfall, but also by the consistent balance of payments deficit. The banks see this coming and use all sorts of tortuous ploys to postpone default because they know the taxpayer will not cough up for another bail-out.

We do not know just how much government debt is held within the banking system today, but in 2009 it was about £200 billion. Add £380 billion of QE (Quantitative Easing) as at this time and make your own guess.

At the start of this chapter we described how banks 'grow' their balance sheets by adding loans to both sides. Why do we not simply demand that they write these artificial numbers off both sides? The answer is of course that it would remove any facade of credibility left in the system, and whilst the top bankers continue to earn obscene bonuses they will continue to resist change.

Perhaps there is another sticking plaster in the political first aid kit, and the fractional reserve will stumble on until the next crisis and another generation of taxpayers and politicians repeat this increasingly painful process. The public debt will continue to grow because it is systemic and therefore destined to end in tears. Fractional reserve is sustained on life support because the payments process is organically integrated into the system along with 97% of the national currency.

That was sufficient for politicians to decree that the banks could not be allowed to fail, or the whole country would collapse. It was a hollow threat but sufficient to persuade politicians to keep it all together in the meantime – at least until it became someone else's problem.

So far the story of banking and finance has been a sorry tale, and by now the reader should be not only bored stiff but thoroughly depressed. But take heart, because from now on it is a journey out of bondage; a road map clearly marked with where we need to go, and the practical means of getting there. We can spell this out, but only people can make it happen.

CHAPTER 12

Why we need our own currency.

Dependency on sterling means dependency upon London - Outlook for sterling - An introduction to the concept of an independent currency as a prerequisite to banking reform - The need to act firmly & early.

The debate on the currency of independence has yet to start in earnest, and having initially ducked this issue with vague remarks about joining the euro, the Scottish government has seized upon sterling as its latest choice of currency following independence. They clearly believe the electorate will be content to leave this key issue unresolved to be dealt with in due course. At the moment there is no point in even considering the euro because Scotland could not join without a two year ERM (Exchange Rate Mechanism) qualification period based upon its own currency – a currency independent of sterling.

The Eurozone countries have a currency union in an ongoing experiment, which will either fall apart, or lead to political union. That is the inevitable outcome for any union of two or more countries which believe they can share a currency and synchronize and manage a common banking and monetary policy – and yet still claim to be independent. Either way, there remain only two options; stay with sterling and the Bank of England, or an independent currency with a Scottish Central Bank.

The Unionist stance remains that Scotland would need to apply for the privilege of joining a sterling area and that this is in the gift of Westminster. We may regard this as political posturing in that we hold a minority interest in sterling, but being realistic our voice would be in the wilderness.

However, from many perspectives Scotland should have a comprehensive strategy to replace sterling at the earliest opportunity.

Not least among these -

- Anyone who considers that sterling is a solid currency has not looked at the balance sheet

- It is not good negotiating practice to be a supplicant with no credible alternative

- The authority to reform and regulate the banking system is a minimum requirement and not an option within a sterling regime.

- Westminster has dithered over Europe since its inception – no one knows if the UK will be in or out within the next few years.

- Only an independent currency opens the door to the prosperity which accompanies full employment and thereby would generate the revenues needed for top class public services and social cohesion.

- No competent business has difficulty with foreign exchange nowadays, it is no barrier to our exports worldwide – including to Euroland.

- The UK trades freely with Ireland and the euro without policed borders. Both Norway and Denmark have their own currencies and experience no difficulties with international trade.

- We would manage our own positive balance of payments a great deal better than Westminster.

Scotland would not wish to see sterling collapse, and this would be aggravated by the loss of Scottish oil to the already disastrous UK balance of payments. At our discretion this blow might be softened by agreeing to sell some oil for sterling rather than for harder currency, and there is a realistic prospect that shale gas will prove commercial all over the UK.

But even so, in the opinion of many, the UK economy is far too dependent upon the alchemy of the City of London. The UK, even with North Sea oil, is dangerously dependent upon 'financial services and markets', and sterling will be extremely vulnerable when, as it surely will, this gigantic bubble eventually bursts and reality comes to the City.

In the run-up to the Referendum, we are familiar with the economic and financial risks of independence – real and imagined, presented by the UK press and media. But it would be naive to believe that doing nothing and remaining financially governed by the proclivities of the Bank of England is a viable option.

What would be likely to happen if an independent Scotland remained with sterling? The UK recently lost its triple A investment status. The only reason the UK has not joined Spain at triple B - just short of junk rating, is because London is the European headquarters of the 'Wall Street Mafia'. There is little else in the art of credit rating to prop up sterling and stave off devaluation, more austerity and mass unemployment. How might Scotland react to this scenario?

The Scottish government could issue its own sterling bonds arguing that they would be 'different' because Scotland has a positive balance of payments and a balanced domestic budget. But foreign currency investors would still suffer the risk of sterling collapse or further devaluation – there would be no difference.

Sterling is a minor and diminishing player in the international borrowing game – its future resting precariously in the hands of unpredictable financial markets.

This same helplessness extends to internal finances – the inability to reign in the private banking system which controls the domestic agenda. If the private banks continue, can Scots Law make them safer and more responsible within Scotland? Let's see....

The banks virtually govern themselves with a modest input from the central banks. The Basel 3 Accord agreed to strengthen capital reserves to some 6% to 7%, although few have conformed so far. In the US the 'Fed' has ruled that major banks there shall hold a minimum of 6% and it remains to be seen if they can effectively enforce this modest recommendation.

Certainly the likelihood of any big bank paying any attention to a new Scots administration is pretty remote. As we know from UK experience, the banks make their own rules, and hold the state to ransom – there being no alternative as Westminster sees it. Whilst Scotland remains in the sterling area there is only one central bank – the Bank of England.

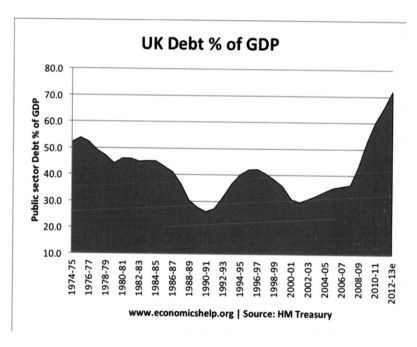

History has proved it has little impact upon the commercial banks, and even if Scotland was permitted a voice on the Monetary Policy Committee it would still be ineffectual. The conclusion must be that nothing would change on the banking front. Over the past thirty years regulators have proved to be toothless tigers passing their time before joining the City club.

So independent monetary policy, while remaining within sterling, is a dead duck in an Independent Scotland. That leaves the much over-egged fiscal powers – the ability to form our own taxation policy. Ranked in economic importance and influence, perhaps ten per cent that of monetary policy. Every reduction in taxation will require an increase take from elsewhere. Rebuilding industry by offering reduced tax to foreign investors is a race to the bottom as other countries follow suit.

We have seen decades of regional tax incentives and grants for job creation and incentives for foreign inward investment – usually multi-nationals which pay little or no tax anyway.

Scotland will be able to balance its domestic budget on present estimates and enjoy all the tax income from North Sea Oil. That is more than can be said for the UK as a whole which has no prospect of reducing its consistent deficits – neither domestically nor in its balance of payments.

Yes, we can stand on our own financial feet, but there will be no oil reserve fund comparable to that of Norway, because the income from the boom years was used to put off the evil day when the UK eventually had to face up to the realities of living beyond its income.

If the 2016 administration is to act responsibly, then our present MSPs must participate actively and openly in this 'What if...' scenario.

The Global Picture

The earlier bullet points will become familiar if the dialogue is permitted to enter the public forum, but an equally important factor is less apparent, and that is the very shaky foundation not only of sterling but of all world currencies – particularly those of western Europe and the USA. To consider this subject in isolation of how best Scotland might protect itself from a much more serious collapse than that of 2008 would leave the job half done.

Although there are many national currencies, they are, with no significant exception, produced by the fractional reserve banking system fully dealt with in Chapter 11. In global terms, all currencies are linked to the US dollar representing the sole reserve currency and pivotal to world trade. They are also inextricably linked through inter-bank lending – highlighted by the LIBOR fraud exposed in 2012.

All have been impacted by the financial crises. The values and ratios of debt below are therefore in US dollars, but the implications are particularly relevant to the UK and sterling, and to a lesser extent the euro. The numbers here are so enormous as to be meaningless to most people, but they must be quoted to justify the unstable ratios of reality to expectation.

(Sources for the following quoted figures: *Office of the Comptroller of the Currency; Economic Policy Journal: Federal Bank of St. Louis; Trading Economics; Treasury Direct; Economic Collapse; Economist.com; The Economist; Global Finance; Wikipedia.*)

- $9,283,000,000,000. Is the total amount of all bank deposits in the United States. The FDIC has just $25 billion in the deposit insurance fund that is supposed to 'guarantee' those deposits. In other words, the ratio of total bank deposits to insurance fund money *is more than 371 to 1.*

- $10,012,800,000,000. Is the total amount of mortgage debt in the United States. As you can see, you could take every penny out of every bank account in America and it still would not cover it.

- $10,409,500,000,000. Is the M2 money supply in the United States. This is probably the most commonly used measure of the total amount of money in the U.S. economy.

- $15,094,000,000,000. Is the GDP, in the US. It is a measure of all economic activity in the United States for a single year.

- $16,749,269,587,407.53. Is the size of the U.S. national debt. It has grown by more than 10 trillion dollars over the past ten years.
- $32,000,000,000,000. Is the total amount of money that the global elite have stashed in offshore banks (*that we know about*).
- $50,230,844,000,000. Is the total amount of government debt in the world.
- $56,280,790,000,000. Is the total amount of debt (government, corporate, consumer, etc.) in the U.S. financial system.
- $61,000,000,000,000. Is the combined total assets, of the 50 largest banks in the world.
- $70,000,000,000,000   Is the approximate size of total world GDP.
- $190,000,000,000,000. Is the approximate size of the total amount of debt in the entire world. *It has nearly doubled in size over the past decade.*
- $212,525,587,000,000. According to the U.S. government, this is the notional value of the derivatives that are being held by the top 25 banks in the United States. But those banks only have total assets of about 8.9 trillion dollars combined. In other words, *the exposure of our largest banks to derivatives outweighs their total assets by a ratio of about 24 to 1.*
- $600,000,000,000,000 to £1,500,000,000,000,000. Is the estimates, of the total notional value of all global derivatives generally fall within this range. *At the high end of the range, the ratio of derivatives to global GDP is more than 21 to 1*

The vulnerability of Global banking is due to minimal reserves and interbank lending as described in Chapter 11. An unstoppable chain reaction is a very real possibility which no finance minister should ignore. It would therefore be prudent to consider here what steps might be taken by a small country to guard against such a disaster invading its economic borders.

Associated with this is the relationship of governments through public debt as witnessed in the Eurozone countries. This creates tensions between States and the meetings of Heads of State, to resolve their financial relationships, does not inspire confidence in concerted action.

The IMF is supposed to be the world authority on international finance, but it too has been exposed as a creature of the banking hegemony. It was created at Breton Woods almost seventy years ago when the USA and UK decided upon the shape of the world's financial system, and its policies still reflect these same political and economic values.

Many people believe the IMF and World Bank to be arms of the United Nations. They are independent and not accountable to the UN although they describe themselves as 'in the United Nations system'. Together with the Bank of International Settlements in Geneva, they are the global face of the present banking hierarchy.

Back in the UK we are assured that such an unstoppable chain reaction may never happen, but that is no reason to avoid considering the consequences if it does, and planning a survival strategy. That means more than cutting the link to sterling and adopting our own currency; it means retaining that currency within our own domestic borders and ensuring that our payments system is never threatened by the paralysis which led to the ongoing taxpayer bail-outs And it means a positive balance of payments on our foreign exchange account and control of exchange rates and capital flows.

It means full reserve banking in Scotland, and the ability to direct our domestic economy to full and gainful employment, and to secure a greater degree of self sufficiency to offset the present over-dependence upon financial markets over which we have no control.

It implies a high degree of diplomacy – the ability to distance ourselves from the centre of a financial tsunami, and yet continue to participate with others who may not see the future as we do. As a small peripheral country we are unlikely to be perceived as a threat to the global financial system and may be looked upon as an interesting working model of an alternative financial culture.

It does not mean trade barriers or protectionism – but it does mean ensuring we are not bought over with worthless paper. It means that if this financial storm breaks we will be ready to batten down the hatches and survive, and if it does not, then we will still be a great deal more secure and better off than most.

Critics argue that an independent Scottish currency would be insignificant and vulnerable. We have dealt with the protection of our currency and need take no lessons from dealers and financial markets. Insignificant – well perhaps in terms of the US and Chinese currencies – certainly – but that is of no more consequence to us any more than to dozens of smaller countries using their own currencies.

Look at Iceland with a population the size of Edinburgh, and able to put the banking genie back in the bottle – more than Washington or London can achieve.

If Scotland does not have its own currency ready, London and foreign owned megabanks, will be firmly embedded into the Scottish political psyche and will remain so after independence. They are part and parcel of the Bank of England and sterling. The Financial Mafia will be installed in Edinburgh, and reform of banking in Scotland will simply not take place.

It has been amply demonstrated over the past five years in particular that bad banking verges on criminal fraud and represents everything that independence is designed to overcome. Every week another bank is fined millions or billions for 'inappropriate' behaviour described as mis-selling or collusion. These apparently huge sums are regarded by the banks as the 'overheads' of financial enterprise, and are dwarfed by what they get away with. Any other individual or business would be charged with fraud and those responsible tried in court and sent to jail. Clearly bankers enjoy a special relationship with the financial law-makers.

London, Brussels, and Washington, have been unable to subdue the dominance of the mega-banks, because once in power they control the democratic process. There is no point in escaping the clutches of the City of London just to fall into the arms of their Edinburgh co-respondents.

That is avoidable if Scotland is fully prepared with its own currency on day one. It is futile to say that this can all be attended to in due course and if found to be necessary. The damage would have been done, the economic citadel already occupied by the fractional reserve banking system, and virtually impossible to dislodge. There is no advantage in an independent currency which is issued and managed by private bankers – we know what that means because it is the state we are in today.

So we must be ready to grasp this unique opportunity to start afresh. The transition from one currency to another may cause a few days of inconvenience, but produce a lifetime of benefit. In the meantime what happens to the pound in your pocket? The present Scottish banknotes require an equivalent value in sterling to be lodged with the Bank of England and of course that will no longer be appropriate. (*Refer to Appendix 5 – Sterling Zone*). As these Scottish banknotes are all denominated in sterling, they will be replaced by new Scots pound notes issued by The Central Bank of Scotland.

The laws would be drafted and ready to be enacted on day one. It is not complicated and the procedure is well proven. Bank balances can be re-designated over a bank holiday weekend and contractual details finalised over the following few months. Scotland would be the 70th Sovereign State to have exited currency areas over the past century with little downward economic volatility.

Let us not invent excuses because the dividends of making the right decision will be enormous. Any inconvenience will be minimal, and the change to a Scots pound pegged to sterling will be the foundation of Independence.

Moreover, although a smooth transition is important, (as detailed in Chapter 15), everyone should remember that in recent years the currency has been manipulated to achieve a political objective – the ascent of the super rich over the democratic process. Here we endeavour to restore the national currency to its proper function – to incentivise full employment, and thereby build up real wealth within the community – surely worth some minor inconvenience compared with the chaos which would follow the potential collapse of your bank.

There is no intention to face down the present global financial order. Rather envisage a small self-reliant nation which will design its own internal financial system in a manner best suited to its needs, and which will interact with its global trading partners individually and responsibly, and in a manner which will not leave it vulnerable to speculation or intrusion.

That means that the central bank will fix exchange rates – an immense advantage possible only if, unlike sterling, there are no holdings of Scots currency outside its own borders. If we start out with that as the law then it can be maintained and foreign exchange rates will be fixed in step with our balance of payments.

Like the NO campaign, the only weapon the bankers have is scaremongering – threats of capital flight, devaluation, economic, and financial breakdown. Ordinary people who know little or nothing about banking and high finance know that this is exactly what is happening now and it is getting worse by the day.

With its own currency Scotland would have a positive balance of payments and avoid the imminent sterling crisis. If we have the nerve to be independent surely we have the common sense to be financially independent too.

Financial independence means restoring accountability to democratic institutions; an end to feeling helpless in the face of banks behaving badly and getting away with fraud and collusion and soaking up billions from taxpayers subsidies and bailouts. An end to government guaranteeing mortgages and business loans because the banks fail to take their proper place in society, and clearing the decks to restore pensions and personal savings ahead of bank profits and bonuses. Last, but not least, capping the huge mountain of public debt which has been allowed to dominate every aspect of economic life.

Why would a newly independent country shoot itself in the foot by adopting someone else's rotten banking system which also controls its currency? With financial independence and our own currency, we can place our money and banks beyond the reach of financial predators and speculators. Every detail of how we do this is covered in the upcoming Chapter 13, (*Constitutional Money*).

Finally we do not know the status of sterling in 2016. It has been depreciating consistently over decades and faces serious public debt challenges. A responsible Scottish government must not find itself being dragged under by sterling default and must have a Plan B up and ready to go on day one – and if it makes it politically more digestible it can be regarded as prudent contingency planning and need not be a state secret. No-one would question the need for an independent Scotland to have effective Defence Forces to protect its on and off-shore assets. Every bit as much it needs to protect its financial system from predators – both domestic and foreign.

CHAPTER 13

Constitutional Money

Constitutional Money - also known as sovereign or plain money, what it is it? - Changing bank credit to plain money. Revisiting the logic of debt relative to public capital investment.

The Constitution of a Nation is the basis of any democracy. It is better set down in writing, but can also exist with less clarity as a set of precedents in law, as in the UK. History has consistently demonstrated the capacity of bankers to acquire control over national monetary systems. If this is to be resisted then there is no option but to enshrine within the Constitution the exclusive prerogative of the State to originate and issue the national currency.

The Constitution is the ultimate sovereign authority rather than the government of the day. The elected politicians who will be responsible for Scotland's written constitution must act to protect themselves and the people from the financial corruption which has undermined our modern western democracies.

Constitutional Money is understood by very few people and at the moment by few who will be present at this first parliament. Left uninformed, there will be a presumption to stay with sterling and take no initiative. If that were to happen, Scotland would be set back many years, perhaps permanently. The public debate must expose the implications that would follow if we stayed with sterling beyond a very short period of transition.

There are three fundamental elements to a sound monetary system – three legs which support a stable platform upon which any number of secondary public functions and private enterprises can be constructed – any or all of which may survive, prosper or collapse, but without threatening the stability of the platform itself.

131

They are -

1. The issue and integrity of the national currency and credit – a Constitutional responsibility of the State.

2. The distribution of that currency among the people and the management of their individual accounts and payments – the responsibility of the chartered banking system.

(**NB**. The provision of investment capital for the private sector is the business of merchant banks, venture capitalists, and the stock market, which are activities above the 'stability' platform described above).

3. Guarding the sovereignty of the currency against attack or corruption – the responsibility of the government of the day.

In developing these headings the Constitution will clearly distinguish between the issue of the currency and its dissemination through the chartered banking system. Although closely related they serve distinct social and economic functions.

The purpose of constitutionalising the origination of the national currency has four purposes:

- First it is to endow the State with the sole right to issue debt free money or money substitutes including bank and electronic credit.

- Second to provide a programme and the means of replacing all existing domestic bank created credit with constitutional money.

- Thirdly it is to furnish the government of the day with the financial means of securing the full and gainful employment of the people.

- Fourth it is to provide a means of capping and reducing public debt. The Constitution will also set down the nature and limitations of these powers.

The underlying philosophy of these proposals is a response to the recognition that productive capitalism and free enterprise have been effectively stunted by the parasitic domination of financial capitalism – the unbridled creation of money and artificial financial structures. Constitutional Money (CM) observes the basic principle that money may no longer be loaned *unless the lender forgoes the use of that money until it is repaid.* Thus only genuine money enters circulation – principally money saved in the past and invested in the future, will provide the bulk of the working capital of the banking system.

There will no longer be M0, M1, M2, M3 & M4. Bank credit will be replaced by liquid sovereign money or CM. This simplifies the entire money system which few understand fully. We all know what cash is and with CM all money becomes cash.

The difference is, that as well as physically exchanging your money, it can now move directly in and out of your electronic wallet or purse – another name for your bank account.

It is not widely appreciated that the money in your present bank account is not yours. It is an asset of the bank which allows you to use its system of debit and credit book-keeping. This is why when there is a run on a bank it goes bust and you lose your money– just as happened with Northern Rock in 2007 and in Cyprus in 2013.

It is also why the government offers limited deposit insurance, and ultimately why banks have to be bailed out by the taxpayer (as described in Chapter 11). With CM none of these props and illusions will be necessary – the banks will no longer issue the money, they will manage your personal and business accounts and cannot even re-lend your money without your consent and a clear contract.

Under the CM system, all money is cash issued by the State, and if everyone suddenly wanted physical cash, then it exists, and there is no magic or illusion involved. In broad principle the nation's stock of currency should be maintained at a level to match its economic activity. That activity will normally be driven by the private sector, engaged in commercial enterprises for the benefit and enjoyment of the whole community. CM is neutral and does not differentiate between economic activities applied to the private or public sector, the criterion is building the wealth and prosperity of the nation.

Constitutional money will also alter the financial concept of public investment, certainly those of an infrastructural nature. The money system would now belong to the community, not the banking corporations.

Whereas at present, government agencies require to borrow from the private banks, they would now access capital funding from the Scottish Investment Bank. This would be free of debt or redemption, as it is expressly not for private profit, but to mobilise the community to create community assets and thereby add wealth to the Nation. Public investment becomes a rational rather than a financial decision.

The changeover is a transparent process which is best described in Chapter 15, where the actual steps of transition from sterling and fractional reserve to CM are set out in some detail.

In this chapter we are focusing on the constitutional aspects of our money system, and at the end of this chapter extracts from a draft version which already exists in the public domain are displayed.

The rate at which new money, or seigniorage, will be added to the money supply by the Constitutional Monetary Authority (CMA) will be governed by considerations of optimizing economic capacity. If performance falls off then it can be directly stimulated by the commissioning of infrastructural or public asset creation; as economic performance rises towards optimum, such stimulus would be withdrawn.

The profusion of bank credit in the past has created an illusion of prosperity whilst the real wealth and creativity of the Nation has declined. That illusion has been stage managed on an unlimited budget and excluded from public accountability. That this is indeed nothing but illusion is witnessed by the collapse and public bail-out of the banking system in 2008.

Banks do not take in and re-lend depositors' money – loans are created and cancelled in a quite separate operation. The loans, credit cards, and overdrafts, which finance the domestic economy are 'credit contracts', only remotely related to the banks' own capital and reserves. The deception has been building for some time - measured by the graph showing bank credit being consistently generated at four times the actual rate of economic growth.

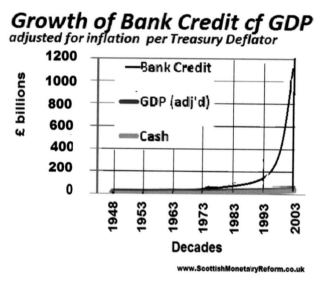

Growth of Bank Credit cf GDP
adjusted for inflation per Treasury Deflator

www.ScottishMonetaryReform.co.uk

There is only one guarantor of a national currency and that is the State. Within that State the confidence, credibility and credit worthiness of its money resides in the integrity of its management and the vibrancy of its economy. To the trading world at large, the balance of payments should be reflected directly in the exchange rates of the currency.

135

These are the proper concerns of all sovereign states, and in particular of those individuals appointed as the trustees of its constitutional money. It may be impossible to effectively outlaw the trading of these sovereign responsibilities in financial markets, but it can most certainly be reduced to manageable proportions by eliminating the National Credit as the primary source of finance for speculators.

To achieve this integrity, all money, be it coin or credit, must source solely and exclusively from the State. The National Credit will not be subject to debt or redemption, and will enter circulation as a replacement of existing bank credit.

Any additional new money beyond this initial issue will be authorised solely by the Constitutional Monetary Authority and earned by the private sector in the course of creating new national infrastructure and public assets. The CMA will enjoy similar status to the judiciary and represents the top tier of the hierarchy (*Refer to diagram in Chapter 14*).

Critics of CM claim that the trustees will authorise too much money and create inflation. That is indeed the pot calling the kettle black. As quantified in the graphic illustration above, the banks have regularly expanded the credit supply many times faster than GDP growth - and created nothing but asset bubbles and inflation.

Constraint upon the issue of new money in any form is obviously essential to stability. The primary constraint upon a fractional reserve bank was perceived as the risk of financial loss to the shareholders if a loan went bad. That risk has been ameliorated by deposit insurance, underwritten by the taxpayer, and provided no constraint upon inter-bank lending.

At Central Bank level various efforts to control lending have proved ineffectual, including relating money supply to growth of GDP, the relationship of the domestic currency to a 'basket of commodities' or various or abstruse statistical indexes, and of course interest rates.

These constraints have failed on two counts. First, they have not restricted the flood of new money into the economy, and secondly, they have institutionalised inflation. The new money has financed no additional public asset which has not been offset by even greater public debt. This is far more than a technical oversight it is a fundamental fault imposing a crushing burden upon the community. It bears repeating that constitutional money provides the sole effective and accountable constraint upon a fiat money system, vulnerable only if the Constitution is violated.

Interest rates have been assiduously promoted as controlling inflation – but they have never done so. Under constitutional money interest rates would not be used to cool an overheated economy – there are far more effective regulators via credit agreement terms, the amount of deposits required, the period of repayment and the like. The primary function of setting basic interest rates will be to encourage and manage the level of private savings invested in the banking system.

Government will no longer borrow the national credit from fractional reserve banks, and no new money will enter circulation which is not earned by productive activity, contributing directly to gross national product. Thus the national debt will be capped and eventually repaid or where held by fractional reserve banks, written off.

Never again will government be held hostage to a private financial monopoly and require to beg private banks to lend to business and industry – the Central Bank would be able, if required, to issue credit directly to the private sector in direct payment for public assets created.

Fiscal policy or taxation is independent of monetary policy, yet the accounting system charges public capital investment against these revenues, but this is not what happens in corporations. Day to day revenues are expected to cover all costs and profit, but new capital investment in buildings and other long term investments are made by borrowing. For a corporation that means long term investment which adds value to the enterprise. CM permits government to use a similar logic by accessing debt free capital for fixed capital purposes – referred to as Fixed Capital Formation.

In 2008 taxation had grown to almost 40% of national incomes[3] of which nearly £40bn was invested in public assets[4]. Little wonder deficits keep cranking up the national debt, adding £31bn per annum in interest charges to the UK tax bill. In 2013 this interest is approaching £50 bn or some 30% of standard income tax – that's where your wages go.

Constitutional money offers the only rational means of reducing public debt, and thus the burden of taxation required to service the interest. Thus future taxation would become available to meet the needs of state pensions and welfare, and to cover the day to day running costs of the administration and public services.

In summary Constitutional Money means that:-

- The State, through the Constitutional Monetary Authority, reverts to being the sole originating authority of the National Currency & Credit

- Public investment is removed from taxation and is funded from seigniorage via the National Investment Bank – PFI without repayment or interest charges

- Equity and democracy restored as the banking sector loses political power and is rehabilitated into the normal economic community

- Government no longer borrows from the banking system. the national debt will be capped; savings and pensions are protected from structural inflation

- Merchant banking will form an entirely separate part of the financial sector – retail banks will no longer be able to use depositors' money for speculation

---

3.   Eurosta Data 2008

4.   Gross Capital Formation (Abstract of Statistics Table 16.21)

Article 6.1: The National Currency & Banking Regulation

6.1.1. The National Currency of Scotland shall be Constitutional Money guaranteed by the State under the Constitution. It shall be the sole legal tender and circulating medium of exchange comprising cash and credit instruments. It will be issued free of debt by the Constitutional Monetary Authority (CMA). The origination or placing into circulation of any other money or money substitute shall be an act of counterfeit.

6.1.2: The primary executive arm of the CMA shall be The Central Bank of Scotland which will originate the currency and regulate its distribution through the Chartered banking system. The Charter shall preclude any foreign national or corporation from the ownership or effective control of any commercial banking institution chartered under this Constitution.

6.1.3: The new currency of Scotland shall be called the Scotmerk and be divided into one hundred pence.

6.1.4. Other than during the transition from Sterling to the new National Currency or in times of National Emergency, no new debt-free Constitutional Money may be created other than as direct payment for the creation of Fixed Public Investment defined here as –

"investment in fixed capital assets in State or community ownership i.e. tangible capital goods or buildings, infrastructure or their replacement after having been scrapped. It is specifically not to directly finance employment, social benefits, tax concessions, consumables or associated expenditures which are defined as charges against public revenues."

For this purpose the CMA shall create a further executive arm – The Scottish Investment Bank. In this capacity The CMA shall be further bound before approving such public investment

(a) To recognize national employment statistics and ensure no adverse impact upon inflation or the productive economy.

(b) To take into consideration any adverse impact upon the National Balance of Payments.

(c) To act at all times to ensure the integrity and stability of the currency

6.1.5 In the exercise of its powers under 6.1.4 the CMA shall be bound to withhold the issue of any new debt free money if
(a) The government fails in its obligations (under 6.2 below)
(b) It detects or forecasts that excessive liquidity in the money supply requires an increase in taxation. In this context the CMA is further required to specify the sum and time scale to be applied.

6.1.6. *In the exercise and function of its jurisdiction, the Constitutional Monetary Authority will be independent of the legislative and executive branches of the Government. Its members will be nominated by a Public Appointments Commission, and appointed by Parliament by a simple majority vote in a secret ballot. The CMA shall be funded by making its own requisition upon the normal revenues of the State.*

6.2 Government Finances & Taxation

6.2.1 Parliament is required to set a balanced budget for the full anticipated term of its administration. On each anniversary the Public Auditor will be required to provide interim accounts and should these indicate a potential deficit the government will be obligated to make a public bond issue for that amount with a one year maturity and make provision for this repayment by an immediate and matching increase in taxation. The government may not issue any other bonds or debt instruments other than as required by the Central Bank in settlement of foreign balance of trade deficit and as limited within its regulation by the Constitutional Monetary Authority.

CHAPTER 14

The Virtuous Circle.

The Virtuous Circle - The hierarchy of institutions of Constitutional Money – keeping the cuckoos out of the nest - The principles and disciplines of financial sovereignty - The methodology of managing the currency - Paying for employment, not unemployment - The role of the National Investment Bank - What constitutes debt free investment? - How does the private sector benefit? - Financing the impact of automation.

It's a tough old world out there, particularly when it comes to money matters. No need to lift your eyes far above the horizon to see the vultures circling. Little old ladies are being relieved of their pensions on a daily basis, and a lot of pretty contemptuous behaviour hides behind a cloak of respectability. On a personal level only the exceptionally astute will have avoided being deceived in financial matters at one time or another. Indeed, when it comes to financial enterprise on the grand scale no one escapes – provided it is on a big enough scale.

Apparently no one sees these things coming – like the latest financial crisis, virtually everyone had lost their money before they were even aware of being robbed. Sometimes we are parted from our money so cleverly and painlessly that again it is difficult to explain how it happened or who took it from us.

Stuff happens, and it is very frustrating not to be able to do something about it. There are two main hurdles to jump if the people who screw us are ever to be stopped. The first is to understand how they operate. That has formed a large part of this book. The second is to reform out financial environment to keep the criminals out – at least the big operators. So we have devised a circle. Inside are the essentials of a sound financial system and

141

outside the forces which would disrupt it. If we define these, our enemies become visible and when we see and understand them, we can defeat them. They are no longer mysterious forces lurking behind smoke and mirrors.

This diagram on page 149 represents the basic monetary elements supporting economic sovereignty and stability - together with the main external influences which can subvert it – Fractional Reserve Banking, and Sovereign Debt.

Within the '*virtuous circle*' a nation state is captain of its own destiny. Its internal finances democratically accountable and its external position periodically adjusted through the rate of exchange – an automatic reality check comparing its performance with other countries. It is a circle to be vigorously defended against self-interested speculators or the political ambition of currency unions. When you turn in for the night you lock the door to keep out unwanted intruders and friends and neighbours take no offence. The same principle applies here.

The dominant myth is that the banking business is global – so interconnected as to be impossible for any single government to influence. De-regulation permitted inter-bank lending, and notional money from the fractional reserve system flowed without restriction across borders and out of the control of national regulators. Once out there in the cyberspace of financial markets the last vestiges of accountability vanished, and the result has been worldwide disruption.

That part of the myth is fact, but the suggestion that no government can do anything about it is a fiction. Certainly for those western governments, infiltrated by Ministers of State and political leaders who are in thrall to the elite, particularly in London and Washington, the prospect of regime change seems beyond the horizon and will be a monumental task. But not for smaller countries, and particularly not for a small nation achieving its independence for the first time and starting with a clean sheet, and as yet, unencumbered with a generation of politicians whose first allegiance is to the City of London.

Scotland therefore stands on the threshold of designing a financial system which reflects the needs of its people, to all its people that is, not just a financial elite. The Virtuous Circle can guide us through how to set about this perfectly achievable task. The first essential is maintaining the integrity of the new currency by enshrining its origination and issue as an exclusive state monopoly under the Constitution.

Now consider the deep red box containing the fractional reserve system and how the currency flows in and out of the circle with impunity, and immediately the State has lost any control over its monetary policy.

Next consider the pink box relating to the situation if imports exceed exports and money is owed to foreigners. When the balance of payments goes into the red the state must borrow from foreign banks and loses sovereignty. If the problem persists the creditors start to buy up your assets or your internal budget comes under strain through interest payments going abroad. The dire consequences of debt are well known in the UK.

If these external factors are isolated the government of the day is freed to exercise democratic power free of the constraints of getting into debt. Decisions are made on rational criteria first, and affordability second. Within the circle we are our own masters, and neither the IMF nor any other external agency can hold the nation to ransom. The currency becomes not just the means of exchange, but the most effective instrument to finance full and gainful employment and incentivise the creation of sustainable wealth within the nation.

Observe the flow of money through the system. The Constitutional Monetary Authority (CMA) receives intelligence from the Statistics Office and other agencies and delegates the issue of the currency to the Central Bank – The National Bank of Scotland (NatBoS). In the early stages, whilst sovereign Constitutional Money replaces notional bank credit as the backing for all loans, NatBoS will debit all the new banks with this matching sum, to be progressively replaced with private savings and investments as old loans mature.

The CMA may also authorise funds directly to the Scottish Investment Bank to finance investment in fixed public sector assets. All funding from the CMA is like cash – free of debt or redemption.

The Constitution binds the CMA to act primarily to maintain gainful employment through capital investment. It cannot authorise new money to pay for, or subsidise, social benefits which are fiscal charges against government revenues. The individuals comprising the CMA will however retain some discretion in defining the terms 'Public Capital Investment' or 'Fixed Asset Formation'. The overarching principle is that no new money may be created which does not directly secure an equivalent increase in public wealth.

Note the phrase public wealth. That is distinct from GDP, a statistic which measures money and that is quite different because banks and governments can print endless quantities of money and pay it out in subsidies, interest, dividends and income, and that will increase GDP but not wealth, which must be tangible and of value to society.

The commissioning of road building, hospitals and schools, public buildings, (but not housing), rail lines and rolling stock, (but only for a publicly owned service), would all be straightforward examples of public capital investment.

Some decisions may however be less clear cut. A practical example might be if a large site were identified where previous use had created such a degree of contamination as to sterilise further occupation. That could be interpreted as creating a capital asset out of a liability, but only if it were then to be put to use for a particular public or private revenue earning purpose.

Or the Defence Department might wish to commission the building of a new warship, and whilst its operational costs would certainly be chargeable to revenue, it might be argued that the vessel itself was a capital investment providing local employment, although it would earn neither a private nor public return on investment.

Retaining these principles is as important, as financial accountability is essential, to good order, and codes of conduct can only make good sense in the context of the times. There can be no doubt that in the future automation will continue to replace labour in both the productive and service areas, and there will come a time when these financial principles will require to be reviewed. Such times are however some way off, and we are only now just beginning to consider that governments should make economic decisions on rational rather than purely financial grounds.

Whilst these reforms will transform public finances, they will impact indirectly upon the private sector. Full employment implies a private sector maintained at or near optimum capacity and a customer base financially able to consume these products and services. That is the basis of building private wealth which in turn generates the prosperity which permits a fair taxation policy.

Private enterprise, by definition, must stand upon its own financial feet, and it will be the job of the banks to provide appropriate working capital facilities on a basis of responsibility and moral hazard which is the skill of a good bank manager lending other people's money. The provision of risk and long term investment capital is not the business of high street banking but of specialised privately owned financial institutions – merchant banks, the stock market and venture capitalists – the latter in the form of companies or individuals. Those who invest in these organisations do so in the full knowledge that they will be accepting a higher rate of risk and return than will be earned investing in the High Street banks and that is how the capitalist system can work to the mutual benefit of society.

Within our Virtuous Circle, we place private sector finance as a distinct function from that of the public sector. We have experienced what happens when the mechanism exists to speculate with other people's money is made lawful and it is for regulators and lawmakers to banish 'chinese walls' and replace them with firewalls.

Automation.

Automation needs more than just a passing reference. Already the cars we drive are made by robots, and CNC machines make a host of consumer products faster, better and cheaper, than human factory workers. Computers have rendered a host of office workers redundant and technology is making increasing inroads into areas previously the domain of the professional and middle classes. It will not be long before software is developed to enable medical diagnosis to be made more efficiently by a computer than by the average family doctor. It is already easier to imagine many of today's jobs which will be displaced by machines over the next ten or perhaps twenty years, than to predict those which remain in their present format.

This was touched upon towards the end of Chapter 5 in Part One, and it is appropriate that we look at the financial complications which this is already inducing into our everyday society. It is a complication which will become a major social problem within a generation.

De-industrialisation

De-industrialisation is the term applied to the closure of plants which cease to be able to compete in the global market place. The term can be extended to include any form of domestic enterprise which is forced to close because its customer base has shrunk due to competition from imported goods and services.

Free trade has long been championed by all industrial nations which prospered from exporting surplus goods and services. An export market also adds volume and advantages of scale which lowers production costs and enhances competitive pricing. The policy condemns protectionism and tariffs as barriers to free trade. In pure commercial terms this is a rational policy.

The policy remains rational for so long as there is a balance of imports and exports between the trading nations. That balance maintains the same logic of any domestic commercial relationship that is earning sufficient income to pay for expenditures and hopefully to make a fair profit.

If however that balance is not maintained and one party builds up a substantial deficit or debt due to the other party, and the prospects of 'catching up' and repaying the debt are remote, then the commercial logic of continuing to do business disappears. This can be distorted if the currency in which the producer is operating is itself being used as a milch cow to drain off regular profits for the elite and is thereby being maintained at an artificially high level

In the absence of commercial logic the case for free trade becomes fatally flawed. That flaw can go undetected for a remarkably long time because the commercial reality which follows upon the non settlement of due debt is not apparent to the commercial parties. The buyer continues to pay the supplier through his banking system and the seller receives the agreed sum, and so the imbalance is of no consequence to the commercial parties and trade continues as usual.

The central banks of both countries do however notice that one is in significant debt to the other. This is called 'Sovereign Debt' and the offices of national statistics present the figures to their respective governments.

The exporting nation wishes to maintain employment and the apparent prosperity of a successful exporting business. The importing nation enjoys getting something for nothing and is happy to instruct its central bank to print bonds (IOUs) in favour of the creditor nation, and pay a modest rate of interest. Both parties are satisfied and the trade continues in the absence of commercial logic.

The replacement of logic by political expediency is made possible by the use of fiat currencies issued by both nations in quantities unrelated to anything real, because paper bonds and notes are churned out through a Central Banking system that requires no ultimate settlement. It may be appropriate here to recall that prior to the last currency which abandoned the gold standard in 1971 (the US Dollar), nations were required to hold gold reserves in order to settle foreign exchange debts.

The replacement of commercial logic by political expediency is not however without a variety of consequences. The non settlement of debt does not mean debt forgiveness. A creditor nation can therefore use its credit to buy up the assets of a debtor nation and will be tempted to do so – provided the debtor nation is not prepared to use, or imply the threat of violence to prevent this.

Among the other consequences of abandoning commercial logic is that eventually the exporting nations expand their industries to a degree far beyond that capable of being supported by the demand of their domestic economy. As other nations follow suit, they too build up a surplus of capacity, which again is unconstrained by commercial logic. Today no politician dare say "No" to the cheap imports from East Asian tigers. Once they were the poor importers of foreign surplus capacity but now they too have abandoned the logic of requiring ultimate settlement.

The domestic consequences of over capacity of course produce their own domestic problems. As firms find commercial survival ever harder they desperately try to cut costs in the name of greater efficiency. First the labour force is progressively reduced followed by financial pressure to 'externalise' as many other costs as possible. That may be a ploy to avoid tax by transfer pricing through a tax haven, or lobbying for a state subsidy as an option to closure and the social cost of unemployment. Or it might be government grants to create new jobs which would otherwise be unviable. It could simply be to liquidate or go into administration. In all cases it is the 'taxpayer' who picks up the bill.

The list of ploys to deal with the absence of fundamental commercial logic is endless, as employers and unions squabble to survive. Finally there is the close down – domestic de-industrialisation. The public feels bemused and let down. Blame is distributed to unions, bad management by employers, lack of national enterprise and of course government. The procedure is to elect a different party to government and the whole process recycles *ad infinitum*. Instead of society improving with each generation it deteriorates to a survival of the financial fittest.

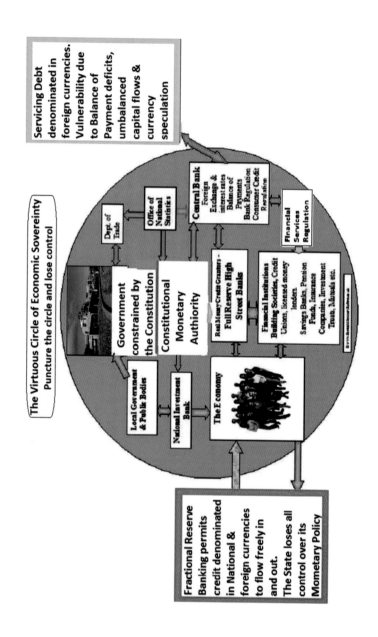

The Virtuous Circle of Economic Sovereinty
Puncture the circle and lose control

Servicing Debt denominated in foreign currencies. Vulnerability due to Balance of Payment deficits, umbalanced capital flows & currency speculation

Fractional Reserve Banking permits credit denominated in National & foreign currencies to flow freely in and out.
The State loses all control over its Mometary Policy

Dept. of Trade

Office of National Statistics

Central Bank
Foreign Exchange & interest rates
Balance of Payments
Bank Regulation
Consumer Credit Regulation

Financial Services Regulation

Government constrained by the Constitution

Constitutional Monetary Authiority

Real Money Credit Granters - Full Reserve High Street Banks

Financial Institutions
Building Societies, Credit Unions, licensed money lenders.
Savings Banks, Pension Funds, Insurance Companies, Investment Trusts, Mutuals etc.

Local Government & Public Bodies

National Investment Bank

The Economy

At present governments duck the issue of unemployment of up to 10%, with the old fashioned neo-liberal responses described in Part One, and in true Westminster tradition, this is a thorny problem best left to the next administration. Here in an independent Scotland, as in Scandinavia, we should be looking at the future more realistically.

It is still doggedly perceived that an ageing population is a financial liability rather than a blessing. It is therefore addressed by increasing the retirement age. That is not because there is work undone which requires to be done; it is because the cost of retirement pensions cannot be absorbed into the present financial system. This problem however also suggests how we might regard the relentless march of automation as a threat, when it is in fact a blessing.

There is a wealth of experience of an older generation which was fortunate enough to retire on what, at the time, appeared to be a comfortable pension. In general, many people were happy to retire at sixty because they could afford to do so. Today there is no good reason why the working population should not be able to retire at fifty five or even fifty. Most would be delighted to enjoy a longer retirement and pursue their hobbies, interests and travel ambitions. The fly in the ointment however is how can we afford that?

The answer to that is the same as the response to unemployment – re-arrange the financial system to serve society rather than to suit self-interested bankers and financial markets. Everyone can enjoy full and gainful employment throughout their active years and live out the remainder in comfort and security. It is perfectly practical and possible even now, but some countries will wait until a desperate population eventually cries enough is enough; others with a little more imagination, enterprise and expertise will manage the transition as seamlessly as the transition from sterling to a Scots currency – the subject of the next chapter.

CHAPTER 15

Transition from Sterling.

Transition is the practicalities and technical process of moving from sterling to the Scotmerk - The experience of other States - Establishing NatBoS – the Central Bank. Reforming the banking system in Scotland - How the man in the street will be effected - Existing contracts, sterling and foreign exchange - Timeline.

Independence Day will be set by the first Scottish Parliament in 2016 and until then, Scotland remains in the UK, and will continue much as at present. Preparation for Independence Day will be undertaken at all levels and at a pace set by the Administration. We will see policies emerging in draft form on every office of government, but there must be a clear over-arching strategy rather than a piecemeal approach, and that means planning well before the event.

If there is co-operation with Westminster this would ideally be phased in over a period of six to twelve months, but the administration must cater for other possibilities – the British State is a notoriously hard negotiator.

A lot of bills will require to be approved in parliament – some in the clear knowledge that they can be fine-tuned at a later date, and some which make a commitment which is likely to be constitutional, and therefore difficult to manipulate after the event. All this should be resolved in the run-up to Independence Day.

That is likely to make the drafting of the Constitution an early item on the agenda, and appropriate currency and banking clauses must be included from the outset. Scotland has its own system of law, but as yet none relative to the regulation of banking and financial services. Just how this could accommodate the banks in

Scotland being subject to English law and regulatory bodies is an anomaly yet to be addressed by the advocates of retaining sterling. This book has demonstrated the corrosive power of the banking and financial system over the democratic process and it is inconceivable that the word 'Independence' could be applied to any country which accepted such external financial governance.

This chapter therefore will confine itself to the introduction of an independent currency and banking system, and the transition from sterling. It will be for parliament to decide the name of the Scots currency, but to avoid confusion with the pound sterling, we shall refer to it here as the Scotmerk – synonymous with one of Europe's best managed currencies, the Deutschmark. The Merk - meaning the mark of silver, was a Scottish coin in circulation prior to the Union.

This is precisely where the otherwise ideal divorce between the Czech Republic and Slovakia encountered its only serious setback. Independence Day had been set for January 1st 1993. The two sides had agreed a currency union based upon the existing koruna.

Within five weeks, speculation and uncertainty was disrupting the settlement of cross border transactions as rumours of the inevitability of separate currencies circulated, and fears of losing out in any devaluation became widespread. Both governments reacted swiftly and agreed to separate currencies – the Czech koruna and the Slovak koruna, and on 8th February all banknotes were recalled to have identifying stamps affixed and were then reissued. Both currencies stood at par on issue, but by August the Slovak currency was trading on forex markets at a 25% discount to the Czech koruna where it settled until Slovakia joined the euro in 2009.

In the previous chapter the desirability of keeping the national currency within sovereign borders was emphasised as essential to avoid currency speculation and financial anarchy. Neither the Czech nor Slovak government had any say on the rate of exchange set by financial markets. Certainly the Slovak GDP per capita was some 25% less than that of the Czechs and that should have prepared the authorities for a rate of exchange differential.

That is not a factor as between Scotland and the rest of the UK as the GDP ratios for both are virtually identical, nor can anyone predict the outcome of the financial and national debt negotiations following Independence. Nevertheless, financial markets thrive upon speculation, and can often induce volatility without rational foundation. The arrangements described to retain the new Scots currency within its borders and the operation of fixed exchange rates would resist such speculation, but these events could affect sterling.

Scotland would enjoy a positive balance of payments as a petro-currency, whereas the UK would continue to operate a balance of payments deficit. Sterling might well fall on forex exchanges simply because political changes might add to quite unrelated concerns over sterling.

The pattern of financial institutions detailed in the Virtuous Circle caters for these conditions and makes the issue of the Scotmerk at par with sterling a sustainable policy – at least until such time as circumstances might dictate a change. Even then, that would be a matter for government to decide and not speculative financial markets.

Those representing the international banking hegemony will oppose these measures vigorously, not because Scotland is a major player, but because they will perceive these moves as the first crack in their power structure.

During the run-up period the new Scottish Central Bank – The National Bank of Scotland (NatBoS), will be established and all commercial banks wishing to continue conducting business in Scotland will require to be identifiable legal entities, registered in Scotland and subject to Scots Law.

Banks will require a banking licence issued by the regulatory arm of NatBoS. So what would be the position of our present banks post independence?

The obvious approach would be to offer the existing Big Banks in Scotland the opportunity to establish subsidiary companies, as legal entities in Scotland, conducting the business of retail banking in accordance with the terms of a NatBoS licence. That, however, would leave the ownership of retail banking and the payments system in Scotland in the hands of the City of London – a hierarchy of private institutions opposed to the principle of Constitutional Money. The business models would conflict at every level and would be incompatible within a subsidiary corporate structure.

This will also be apparent to the present management and shareholders who would in any case be unlikely to meet Article 6.1.2 of the Constitution .... *"The Charter shall preclude any foreign national or corporation from the ownership or effective control of any commercial banking institution chartered under this Constitution"*.

An alternative would be for the Scottish government to offer to purchase the tangible (non financial) assets of the five main banks in Scotland at a fair price, engage all staff, and take over existing active current and savings accounts.

These customer accounts and corresponding liabilities would be removed from the balance sheets of the present banks and transferred to the new state-owned banks.

In the unlikely event of the banks being unwilling to sell, this could still be achieved, with the goodwill of tens of thousands of skilled bank employees in Scotland. They are more aware than most that only a tiny handful of the super-rich comprise the banking hierarchy of CEOs and directors who pay the political lobbyists, PR companies, and trade bodies, which control the banks and financial markets.

No one knows if the efforts of the Westminster government will succeed in re-privatizing RBS, but if this was still publicly owned in late 2014, it could figure prominently in negotiations. The huge RBS campus at Gogarburn in Edinburgh would provide excellent accommodation for the NatBos, and up to a third of the branch banking structure needed for commercial banking in Scotland. Foreign and non-core assets would be sold off.

For an indefinite period the banks will be owned and managed by the State, although as soon as the new system is established and bedded down, the banks will return to private hands – either as a number of smaller privately owned units or as mutuals owned by the customers and members.

As with the current publicly owned RBS, there will be little outward change for the customer. However, these will be matters to be formalised during the interregnum between Independence Day One, with the election of the first full Scottish Parliament since 1707, and Independence Day Two when all the official trappings of power complete their transfer from Westminster.

Independence Day Two will also be independent currency day. Over the ensuing bank holiday weekend all bank accounts and debts will have been re-designated in scotmerks, and sterling will cease to be legal tender in Scotland.

An older generation will recall a similar arrangement when sterling went decimal in 1971. For an undefined period in excess of thirty days sterling and merks will remain pegged at par by NatBoS. One Pound Sterling, equal to one Scotmerk, which will be divided into one hundred pence. The banks will have been issued with new notes and coins denominated in scotmerks, and from the Tuesday following the bank holiday, Bank of England and Scots banknotes designated in sterling may be exchanged at par value for the new notes.

Sterling notes and coins will remain interchangeable for a further 30 days and thereafter will be withdrawn from circulation and not re-issued. During this 30 day period, sterling will not be legal tender but will be recognised as an acceptable means of payment, although people may retain as many sterling notes as they wish.

All commercial banks will have accounts with NatBoS. As banks may no longer create their own credit, all loans and overdrafts will now be funded from this account. This is a seigniorage account, and will have been credited with the new notes and coins provided by NatBoS to the bank, and will also be credited with the amount of existing credit issued by the bank to its customers in loans, mortgages, or overdrafts etc. These credits will of course be liabilities of the bank. As these loans are repaid the banks will be expected to fund new loans from savings, pension and investment funds.

For most Scots used to Scots banknotes there will be little difference to notice; instead of a five pound note bearing the ciphers of one of the Scottish commercial banks there will be a Five Scotmerk note from The National Bank of Scotland. Instead of price labels showing £9.75 it will be SM9.75 or perhaps S_m9.75.

From Independence Day 2, all new commercial contracts will be denominated in scotmerks. Existing contracts denominated in sterling will remain enforceable in sterling following a simple form of registration with NatBoS. Securities held by individuals and financial asset managers will continue to be bought and sold freely on international stock markets, and commercial banks will settle these just as other commercial transactions in foreign currencies.

The present British banking establishment will of course oppose these changes at every opportunity saying it will lead to chaos, it will be too expensive, they will not receive sufficient private investment to make loans and mortgages, and it is all too complicated to make the switch, and it will not work. Well of course they would say that, and you may depend their scaremongering will be really, really scary. If it were not so, then these reforms would not be doing their job.

In fact the changes are minimal. Customer accounts are unchanged and service to customers is significantly improved. Instead of charging customer loans to an internal account they are simply charged to an external account with NatBoS. Instead of dealing using their own or an independent forex market dealer, they will use NatBoS. Nor will the banking Establishment welcome new company laws designed to give small shareholders more than a nominal voice in at the AGM, or a fresh look at how the auditors will be obliged to tighten up on non-performing loans, and be precluded from acting as consultants as well as auditors to the same client, or how new laws will clarify the flexible boundaries between tax avoidance and evasion.

We have no banking statistics for Scotland, but taking the whole of the UK there are over 38 million savings accounts in a population of 63 million and over £4000 billion is invested in saving, pensions and securities. Sterling bank loans to individuals and businesses were substantially less than half this amount in 2009, so it is a safe conclusion that Scots too would be happy to invest safely for a reasonable return.

When considering the volume of available savings relative to the demand for bank loans, it is useful to keep in mind that prior to the demise of the building societies in 1986, these mutual institutions provided virtually 100% of all UK residential mortgages, and were fully funded by members' savings. Mortgages represent some 75% of all lending in the UK. (*See Appendix 1*).

Scotland will be as supportive of business and enterprise as any nation, but it will also promote a fair and open business ethos. This will disadvantage none but those who seek to exploit the society which supports them. Debates on alternative tax systems which resist corporations 'externalising' their own costs on to the public exchequer should be an early priority. Scotland should earn a reputation for a fair and equitable society for rich and poor alike.

Foreign Currencies.

Behind the scenes the banks will have prepared their accounting and payment card systems to adapt to the new currency. Although pegged to the scotmerk at par, all sterling transactions will now require to be registered at NatBoS as a foreign currency, just as the euro or Norwegian krone. And, incidentally, just as the present Scots pounds have to be registered at the Bank of England.........

A sterling payment or receipt will be as straightforward as it is today. Anyone who has made an online purchase knows that bank transactions are already fully automated. A payment in US dollars or euros is instantaneously converted at the current exchange rate, debited to your account in your own currency and credited simultaneously in the seller's account. It is the same when using an ATM abroad.

These programmes will be modified to route the transactions to your bank's master accounts with NatBoS to record and convert the forex transaction. NatBoS will categorise forex movements by size and frequency, and will issue identity codes to traders making or receiving frequent payments

The scotmerk will not be freely convertible, and foreign exchange rates will be fixed by NatBoS from time to time in the course of balancing the terms of international trade. NatBoS will provide the basic foreign exchange service to licensed commercial banks, and thus the scotmerk will not feature in financial or foreign exchange markets outside Scotland. Individuals and corporations may own unlimited volumes of scotmerks, but the system belongs to the people of Scotland, and will be managed in their interests before all others. Scotland will earn foreign currencies from its exports and pay for its imports from these earnings, and thus it will not be possible for speculators to trade or threaten the value or integrity of the Scotmerk.

This is simply explained because in order for a currency to be traded – usually electronically, the seller requires to be able to buy it in the first place and deliver it in the second. If the only legal source of Scotmerks is NatBoS, then buying or selling in another currency is not possible. Any attempt to circumvent this law would lead to the transaction not being recognised by NatBoS. Deals within Scotland could not be enforced under Scots law, as only the scotmerk is legal tender in Scotland.

Similarly as all foreign currency transactions require to flow through NatBoS, it will be possible to ensure that domestic monetary policy is not disrupted by external financial interests transferring large sums of money around the world seeking the best interest rate returns.

These arrangements make it unnecessary to impose conventional capital flow controls. The exchange rate will be pegged to sterling for at least thirty days and residents will face no restrictions against holding sterling or any other currency in accounts administered outside Scotland.

Funds from such accounts may be remitted back to be credited to domestic scotmerk accounts without restriction, but after the thirty days such repatriation may be subject to exchange rate fluctuation – up or down. The only exception will be a limit of 500 scotmerks being taken out of the country in cash in any one year. This is because each time a scotmerk leaks across the border it takes a little bit of financial sovereignty with it. This is, however, unlikely to cause any inconvenience to travellers because credit cards and electronic transfer now constitute the primary means of domestic and foreign transactions, and these will remain unrestricted.

Interest rate policy

The history of using interest rates as an economic policy tool has been abysmal, mainly because it affects financial markets and moneylenders rather than the real economy. Certainly they affect personal borrowing and repayments, and make budgeting a matter of guesswork. Stability within a constitutional money regime is best achieved by relating interest rates to demand for loans and inflation.

Savings and pension funds are key to funding a full reserve banking system –they are the primary source of all institutional lending, and NatBoS will pitch interest rates at a level to attract investment from these sources, perhaps between four and five per cent. This would suggest lending rates averaging five to seven percent for collateralised loans such as mortgages.

It is possible to set interest rates at levels to suit the economic environment in Scotland without the influence of external financial markets because our domestic currency would be protected from speculative deposits and withdrawals from abroad by the 'filter' provided by NatBoS foreign exchange policy.

Inflation controls

It is not anticipated that interest rates will figure prominently in rebalancing an underperforming or overheating economy.

Adjustments to consumer credit mechanisms (minimum deposits and repayment periods etc.), would be more widely applied to fine tune the domestic economy and have been proven in the past to act swiftly and effectively. The main factor influencing economic activity will be by adjusting the pace of commissioning public investment and rates of taxation.

Clearing Payments

As the scotmerk is a liquid asset guaranteed by the State, cheques and electronic transfers will no longer be required to 'clear' between banks as all transfers will be directly recorded between the relative accounts.

It may be recalled that the clearing process is peculiar to the fractional reserve system wherein the IOUs of participating banks were netted and interbank balances adjusted on a daily basis. As CM, in all its forms is legal tender, just as is cash, so this cumbersome process is no longer required. Instead, on clearing payments through the APAC system, all account balances will be reconciled with the State Seigniorage account, thus ending private bank credit creation.

Deposit Insurance

The law on constitutional money guarantees you own the money in your bank account. At present the bank owns your account because it appears as an asset in its balance sheet, hence the taxpayer guarantee of up to £85,000. Under constitutional money, all the money in your account is already registered with NatBos, so if the bank goes bust you will not lose your money – the administrators would simply move your account to another bank.

How will banks be funded?

As it will no longer be legal for a bank to create credit simply by adding the loan to both sides of its balance sheet, so its existing lending will be funded through its account with NatBoS. This will be a temporary facility reducing as existing loans are repaid and new loans are funded by private investors or, in the case of mutuals, by members. The rate of interest charged to banks on this facility would be nominal, as the object is to stop private credit creation rather than raise the cost of borrowing.

There will be several classes of investment accounts, e.g. pure, current and savings accounts, where, in each case no part of any of the balances will be loaned out. These will attract a very low or nil interest rate. Other investment accounts will be used wholly or in part for lending and carry interest rates according to the selected level of risk. Secured mortgage lending would have a low risk/return ratio (as were the pre 1986 building societies), whereas a new business seeking working capital or overdraft might be classed as high risk.

It will be for individual banks to offer such deals but in all cases they would be spread over a very large number of investors and only called upon if an unusually large number of bad debts exceeded the normal level of bank reserves. Investment in retail banking would enjoy the low risk profile of gilt-edged securities which will be gradually phased out as they mature.

Security

Quite apart from day to day criminal fraud, modern money in any form is vulnerable to systemic cyber attack, and contingency plans should be ready for such an event. This requires an adequate supply of cash to be swiftly available in note form. Unlike normal everyday cash, these additional notes would be validated by NatBoS only in such an emergency, and made available to all banking outlets. The validation condition renders the storage of such a large sum of cash secure from any incentive to illegally obtain or use the notes. Similarly facilities would be retained to handle a large volume of cheques until conditions returned to normal.

Conclusion.

Our present UK money system is a complete shambles. Parliament is on a treadmill worrying about money matters and driving the rest of us through hoops to satisfy the banking community – fiddling while Rome burns. Surely we have all had enough of this. It doesn't work for you or for me or for 99% of the community.

We have looked at this nonsense in some considerable depth here. We know what's wrong and how it can be fixed. As it stands, our parliaments have licensed a money system which has turned on them and us, but they must bite the bullet and take back the powers they have unwittingly given away. That it is difficult to do so, simply confirms just how powerful the money system is, and how dangerous to our liberties it has become in the hands of the greedy and unscrupulous. Hard to accomplish when that power is in effective control, but an independent Scotland would be in a position to stop it before it took root.

There can be no better cause to fight, but where are the champions? Well don't waste your time in Westminster or Whitehall, for you will not find them there. But you might just find a readymade army on the streets of Glasgow and Edinburgh, and in every town and village in Scotland.

They are out there waiting to be convinced that Independence would infuse a new sense of purpose and identity to who they are. The same sentiments invoked in that famous extract from the Declaration of Arbroath can today be targeted at the oppression of the bankers. The second version substitutes only Bank for King and The City of London for The English.

The Original 1320 Version -

*"Yet if he should give up what he has begun, and agree to make us or our kingdom subject to the **King of England** or the **English**, we should exert ourselves at once to drive him out as our enemy and a subverter of his own rights and ours, and make some other man who was well able to defend us our **King**; for, as long as but a hundred of us remain alive, never will we on any conditions be brought under **English** rule. It is in truth not for glory, nor riches, nor honours that we are fighting, but for freedom – for that alone, which no honest man gives up but with life itself".*

The 2014 Version

"*Yet if he should give up what he has begun, and agree to make us or our kingdom subject to the* ***Bank of England*** *or the* ***City of London****, we should exert ourselves at once to drive him out as our enemy and a subverter of his own rights and ours, and make some other man who was well able to defend us our* ***Bank****; for, as long as but a hundred of us remain alive, never will we on any conditions be brought under* ***City of London*** *rule. It is in truth not for glory, nor riches, nor honours that we are fighting, but for freedom – for that alone, which no honest man gives up but with life itself*".

Endpiece

The foregoing chapters are a mix of historical fact and future stratagems. Both are open to interpretation and criticism of bias – that is in the nature of all writing. Where new ideas and methods are proposed we believe they are practical and achievable – given the political will.

In this end piece however we allow ourselves the freedom of fantasy. It is included for all those many people who want more information on 'Independence' but who find it hard to ask specific questions.

Financial Advisors and neo-liberal economists do this regularly, as does the fortune teller at the fairground. The wise client expects nothing, and is seldom disappointed. On the other hand, a little imagination can stimulate interesting questions....

Closer to home and for the present anyway, Westminster is embarked upon a war of words and propaganda, aimed at undermining the confidence of the Scots in their ability to run their own government; they maintain that Scotland would be an economic disaster area which, in the current circumstances, is a bit like the kettle calling the pot black. Nevertheless, if we ignore the lesson of Czechoslovakia and fail to have our currency house in order, then we are little better than our critics..

Looking into the crystal ball, if the vote is for 'no change' then the outcome is predictable. The UK will continue upon its present path and the Scots will remain passengers on the Westminster train of ineffectual crisis management. The debt and taxation burden will escalate as we hurtle towards the buffers.

The End of Empire is a slow withering process, but of course the UK still has a future. It is however a future dictated by others. The leaders in Westminster are not carving out a future; they have dug a grave already half full of discarded industries and the detritus of economic failure.

England will survive, but is now just the latest name to be added to other empire builders of the past, Greece, Italy, Spain and Portugal. As with these once illustrious nations, the corruption starts at the centre and even the most ardent Unionist must recognize the signs.

The City of London is a focal point of the ongoing financial crisis, yet it is perceived as the corner stone of the UK economy - a triumph of shadow over substance. The outcome is certainly predictable.

The national debt is unsustainable, with no credible Treasury policy to contain it, and the balance of payments has a disastrous accumulation of foreign debt, which is consistently growing with every annual deficit. This is a paper tiger economy out of control.

Conversely the pro-independence groups see the future differently. The United Kingdom is our country as much as anyone else's, and the Scots have integrated happily with their English, Welsh, and Irish cousins. We do not see independence as separation or the breakdown of personal relationships. We perceive it more as the nascent entrepreneur giving notice to his employer and setting up his own business. No hard feelings, he just believes he can do things better and without the baggage of past glories. Having decided to go after 300 years our family ties will continue to bind us together across an invisible border and we will remain bound together as people - if not politically, then certainly as friends and relations.

So what will be different in Scotland if it were to become independent? Let us assume that for all the scaremongering and tales of woe, the British State accepts the outcome of the 2014 referendum as a clear vote for independence and approaches the negotiations even-handedly and with goodwill.

The Scottish government is unlikely to call a general election until the scheduled date in 2016. The outcome of that election may well be a coalition of familiar names but now, for better or worse, all committed to Scotland as a Nation again.

If we are going to forecast the future in a broad sense, let's skip all the political machinations of who gets what job, and the mechanics of transferring the trappings of power and negotiating who gets what and when – all that is process and, inevitably it will take time. It is likely to be well into 2017 before the dust settles and Scotland adopts her new identity.

By that time there will have already been some exciting events – the Commonwealth Games will have been and gone, leaving a legacy of administrative successes in the sporting arena for Scotland, which has matched the extensive new facilities and revitalized coaching attitudes.

It is Monday 7th September 2020. The radio alarm announces

the 7 o'clock news. "Good morning. This is Radio Scotland". You could still have tuned into the BBC if you wanted to but Scottish Broadcasting now runs the National broadcasting and TV channels. Like the BBC it is funded by government but watched over by a much more open and accountable Trust.

The news is certainly more local "The Minister for Transport will officially open the new M9 motorway between Perth and Inverness on Friday. This is five years ahead of schedule and the remainder of the motorway to Aberdeen is expected to complete by 2025 also five years ahead of the original plan. These projects form part of the capital works programmes financed under the government's debt-free Constitutional Money Authority." You know we have the people and skills to achieve this, and having read Part Two you will also know how it was financed.

Over the rush of the shower you hear, "Official statistics issued yesterday show Scotland to be enjoying almost full employment levels other than in a few isolated urban pockets which are proving difficult to clear up. However, continuing skill shortages still hamper a construction industry experiencing its greatest demand for fifty years".

In the kitchen you hear the post dropping through your letterbox, and you recall when the Scottish Government, by a huge majority, warned prospective purchasers of the Royal Mail that these services and assets would be renationalised at the earliest opportunity, and any compensation would be limited to Scotland's share of the privatisation proceeds. That difficulty was resolved by emergency legislation, which devolved postal services in Scotland pending formal completion of the independence negotiations.

The newsreader is still rabbeting on, "King Charles will formally open the next Scottish Parliament in 2021". This will be the first royal visit since the referendum on the monarchy two years ago, when Scotland voted by a 35% majority to join the British Commonwealth. This was hotly debated at the time, and the outcome is widely considered as being influenced by the argument that the Union of the Crowns in 1707 rendered the tradition of the monarchy as much part of Scottish history as it was that of the English.

This decision to join Australia and Canada in the Commonwealth meant that the King's head remained on the coins and notes of the Scots pound which replaced sterling in 2016. (It is officially called the Scotmerk, but most people refer to it as the Scots pound). The Scots pound had been pegged to sterling for almost twelve months but was now at a 12% premium over sterling. The National Bank of Scotland had been obliged to adjust the exchange rate after a significant drop in sterling following further banking scandals and further decline in the balance of payments in the English economy.

Anyway, breakfast over you go outside and get into your electric car. You like to keep in touch and switch on the radio. You wince as you hear that a few dozen more innocents have been killed in Middle East incidents and that British troops are being readied to join the latest conflict in Pakistan.

You leave your car in the underground car park below the station and take your seat in the sleek new Scotrail unit. It was designed for the new high-speed network due to connect into your area within the next two years but hey there, that's what happens if you live in the country.

There are fewer cars on Glasgow's streets than there used to be and you hop on to one of the free trams which silently ply the city streets. Edinburgh eventually got its trams way back in 2014, but Glasgow now has a more modern tram system. So another day at the office... Oh yes, there are fewer shops in a more concentrated city centre, but contrary to some pundits, home working has not replaced the office yet.

This is a clean modern city, and its clean and well maintained because independence is transforming social attitudes to work. The guy, who drives the electric street cleaner, and the young tradesmen painting that shop front, enjoy the same social status as your colleagues in the office. Because the job they do is equally important. The City is no longer run down and shabby because the Council can now afford to employ the people they need, and pay decent wages.

Independence has already produced a different attitude to the old British class system. Technical colleges produce graduates in what used to be called 'trades' and welders and plumbers use modern technology as effectively as anyone else in this more equal and fairer society.

Full employment is almost here, and even now the changes are clearly visible. If public works require to be done and the labour and materials are available, the work gets done. We don't hear that old nonsense about us not able to afford it, while keeping people out of work. Anyway we pay out far less of our taxes in social subsidies and unemployment benefits now.

Out in the countryside nothing much seems to have changed but new legislation is in the offing to introduce land taxes which promise to reform the relationship between large landowners and tenant, and to strengthen the authorities having responsibility for wildlife, putting stewardship before ownership.

New foreign exchange rates have taken effect and some items of clothing and footwear are not just as cheap as in the old days – maybe up ten per cent, but a lot more stuff is made in Scotland, and food, well that is plentiful and from all over the world.

Farming and fishing are getting back to the good old days and there is a quiet satisfaction all round that we produce more of what we eat and wear – not because we must, but because the quality is better and it makes us feel good and creates useful and well paid employment, while helping the environment.

You leave the office early as you have an appointment with your bank manager. He is located in one of the many new Mutual Banks which have opened up in recent years on the High Street.

You and the family are having a special holiday so you want to sort out the finance. A short chat and he sorts it out. You will be flying from Glasgow and have noticed the increasing number of direct flights to and from Scotland – just like Norway and Denmark – fewer queues and frustration at gigantic 'hubs'.

Still, it's good to hear that agreement has at last been reached for Scotland to build a high speed rail link to Carlisle – hope the English keep their promise to complete their end on time. There seems to be a constant increase in travel between England and Scotland nowadays – there never have been any restrictions, it is simply down to greater prosperity, and of course the rate of exchange now makes everything south of the border that much cheaper. Perhaps the novelty of visiting friends and relations living 'abroad' in the old country also adds to the experience.

Many more people now visit Scotland and visiting facilities have improved a lot. This is probably down to initiatives like the new Scottish Film and Television College. This has a huge studio facility, equipped with all the latest technology, and is rented out to private sector producers from all over the world. This is proving not only a great incentive to local talent but a useful foreign currency earner.

Scotland, like Scandinavia is not a 'cheap' destination for visitors, but the tourist business has been very much upgraded into the 21st century since independence.

Ideas like this never used to get off the ground – usually scuppered by lack of money for community developments which would not generate enough profit. Now there is the Public Environmental Initiative whereby local authorities can apply for debt-free money to improve and add to local facilities. Along the Clyde coast old piers are being refurbished and another vintage steamer is to be added to the Waverley fleet. But it's not all heritage and museums displaying past glories. Moves are afoot to reintroduce commercial shipbuilding on the Clyde and managers have already been visiting Finland and Germany to catch up on the renewal of old skills.

On the subject of ships and boats, the earlier generations of redundant nuclear submarines were removed from Rosyth at the end of 2017, from which base the Scottish Navy now maintains its primary responsibilities in the North Sea. Plans for a major new university campus at Faslane, including the Nautical and Armed Forces Colleges, and a naval facility, are well in hand, and work is scheduled to start immediately after decontamination.

Out in the wider world and following her maiden speech at the United Nations Assembly, the Secretary General had warmly welcomed the Scottish representative. He congratulated both Scotland and the U.K. on negotiating this agreement as a significant contribution to world peace and the UN campaign for nuclear disarmament. He looked forward to Scotland featuring prominently in all aspects of the work of the assembly.

These are mostly all 'things' which are naturally important. Harder to put into words is the refreshed sense of identity and purpose now apparent among the vast majority of people in Scotland. We have left a regime which no longer suited us, and are once again Scotland's people.

We twa hae run about the braes,
and pu'd the gowans fine;
But we've wander'd mony a weary fit,
sin auld lang syne.

And there's a hand, my trusty fiere
and gie's a hand o' thine
And we'll tak a right gude-willy waught
for auld lang syne

Robert Burns

APPENDICES

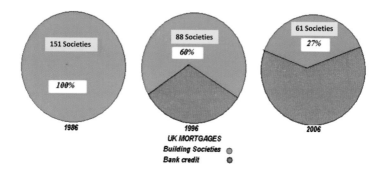

Now observe this remarkable coincidence of how house prices have moved before and after this event.

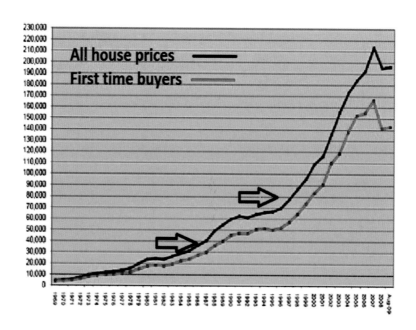

1. The Great Housing Bubble

When Mrs. Thatcher and Keith Joseph pulled the trigger on the Big Bang, the building societies were either bought over by the big banks or in a few cases became banks themselves. This was trumpeted as competition to benefit the consumer. This wee pie chart on the oposite page shows how the societies, which, up until 1986 funded the entire UK mortgage business, were emasculated by the banks over a period of ten years.

All those years just moving up with inflation, then the banks come on the scene, savings are replaced with credit and the sky's the limit – until it all goes pear shaped – not real alchemy at all, just another banking illusion.

2. FAQ – About Fractional Reserve Banking

Q You advocate full reserve banks – what's wrong with the present fractional reserve system?

A This is not widely understood and is best answered by a diagram – (*See opposite page*)

Q. Why is an independent currency so important?

A. Because using someone else's currency binds you to their financial ethics – essentially their banking **regulations**. Scotland will need a stable banking system and public investment based on need and not perpetual borrowing.

Q. Where is this extra money to come from?

A. Exactly where it comes from at present – the people – our savings, investments and pensions, will be the core of the banking system. The vast bulk of UK lending (75%+) remains residential mortgages and until 1986 funded entirely by building societies which were full reserve institutions.- until acquired by the banking system using 'notional credit'.

UK household savings & pensions in 2009 were £4,024 billion – more than twice total bank loans and mortgages.

Q. What if savers are not prepared to invest in the banks?

A. It is up to the banks to make it an attractive investment. Government will provide additional credit. But the government would always step in if necessary.

Q. Ah! You contradict yourself – you condemn 'printing money' but advocate precisely that! How is that justified?

A. Printing money to bail out banks or rescue any other private enterprise is theft from the people by inflation. Printing money exclusively to finance public building & infrastructure does not dilute the currency – it ensures full private sector employment to build wealth.

The Constitution will require <u>all</u> new money to enter circulation as direct payment from the Central Bank for the creation of tangible public assets and only then will the money be paid into the banking system.

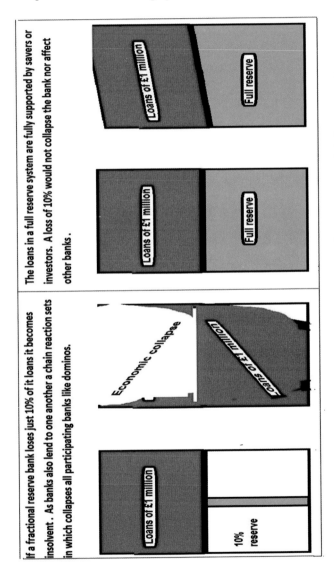

The two main banking systems - Fractional Reserve and Full Reserve - Stability comparison

Q. Can this contribute to financial stability without impinging upon the rights of the individual and the capitalist system?

A. Some freedoms must be restricted by law – the right to murder, steal and defraud. No currency regime can be stable if credit money can be produced for private advantage – either legally as with banks, or illegally by counterfeiters. That is why Fractional Reserve Banks are outside the 'Virtuous Circle' Only a stable money system will optimise the exchange of goods and services essential to building real, sustainable wealth. That is genuine capitalism.

Q. How will full reserve banking prevent financial manipulation?

A. The new Banking Charter precludes creating credit or lending more than the bank holds in its reserves. Trading in securities and the securitisation of primary debt will be disallowed thus preventing speculating using money guaranteed by the taxpayer.

Q. What is securitisation?

A. Selling your loans and mortgages to the financial markets.

Q. Will all this stop 'boom and busts'?

A. Individuals may still collectively contribute to 'bubbles' by speculation or gambling and that should not be prevented but the consequences can be restricted to the participants by requiring all such 'investments', and short selling, to be on a cash up front basis.

Q. All very well in theory but clever people have always managed to manipulate the money business – how can that be forestalled?

A. It cannot, but effective regulation can keep it within bounds. The principle that money is the means of creating real wealth, and not wealth in itself, requires to be enshrined in the Constitution. Other laws will incorporate changes in Corporate Governance whereby shareholders will be empowered to exercise more influence over the policy of large corporations. The balance between irresponsible greed and responsible enterprise requires to be restored, and the definition of financial fraud extended and recognised as anti-social behaviour.

Q. The controls upon capital flows across borders are directly opposed to the current 'open border' global investment policy supported by the EU, WTO and IMF. Will this not isolate Scotland?

A. Cross border capital always flows into the cheapest source of labour and resources thus emasculating the ability of the nation state to influence its internal affairs – that must always be unacceptable to a democratically elected government. Nor can full reserve banking operate in a currency regime alongside 'notional' credit. Scotland is nimble enough to avoid being bullied.

Q. Why advocate exchange rates fixed by the Central Bank rather than the open market?

A. Initially the Scots merk will shadow sterling, just as the Danish krone shadows the euro, but it is the responsibility of the Central Bank to maintain its balance of payments – not a financial market driven by speculation. When that is stabilised the peg can be removed. Fixed rates also ensure flexibility in the interpretation of protectionism, free trade and fair international competition. (*See 'Virtuous Circle diagram.*)

Q. Would Scotland have a positive balance of payments'?

A. Yes. For many years the UK has run a consistent deficit accumulating at the rate of £50/60 billion per annum. That is why sterling is a weakening currency. Scotland would have a comfortable surplus. As a petro-currency the Central Bank would control exchange rates such that the merk did not rise to a premium which might disrupt normal trading relationships.

Q. What will be the main difference be for bank customers?

A. Very few – the relatively recent experience of the change to the euro was almost seamless and the novelty wore off within a few days. Sterling payments will be automatically converted to merks when credited to your account – just as any payment in euros or dollars is presently converted to sterling. Similarly payments instructed in a foreign currency will be debited to your account in merks and transferred in the appropriate currency. Visitors using their credit cards in Sterling or Euro Area ATMs will find their accounts debited in their own currency – just as at present. All banks wishing to conduct business in Scotland will require to comply with their charter – a licence issued by the Scottish Central Bank to appropriately qualified businesses.

Q. Will the changes affect other financial services?

A. Securities denominated in foreign currencies, including sterling, will require to be registered in the name of the beneficial owner – nominees will not be recognised under Scots law. The reason for this is to prevent unauthorised capital transfer but is also linked to the new laws on corporate governance enhancing the rights of shareholders. The regulation of companies dealing in insurance, managing investments and pension funds etc. are unlikely to be materially affected as these perform a socially useful function unrelated to financial manipulation.

Q. Is it likely that the Scottish Stock Exchange will be reinstated?

A. Yes. Ideally it would be structured to raise private capital for commercial enterprises with share trading as a secondary function. It would be regulated to preclude short selling or a platform for potentially disruptive speculation.

Q. How would an Independent Scotland (IS) have bailed out RBS and HBoS?

A. This is a hypothetical question because an IS would have quite different banking laws which would not permit retail banks to act as investment banks. High street banks or retail banks and building societies would be smaller and more numerous.

If these banks had still been operating in an IS (perhaps during the interim until the new banking regime was fully functional), they would have been placed into administration ensuring continuity of retail banking and the payments system. The retail operations were profitable and the losses were due to acquisitions and speculation by the non-retail divisions – investment banking. If selling off these non retail net assets was insufficient to make the residual retail division solvent then the Central Bank would have provided the necessary working capital – a very modest sum relative to the enormous toxic loans and liabilities of the non-retail divisions.

Q. Would an IS force existing UK banks to break up into smaller units?

A. All banks wishing to operate in Scotland would require to conform to the Law of Scotland. That means they must be an identifiable legal entity which comply with the law.

Q. What would an IS do if the banks refused to agree?

A. No individual or corporation is above the law. In such an event the government would nationalise all the banking assets with fair compensation provided the banks co-operated. If the banks refused to co-operate and chose to confront the elected government then they would be nationalised without compensation and all bank employees in Scotland would become employees of the State. Temporary legislation would freeze all assets and liabilities of the subject banks pending settlement negotiations. An IS would not find itself hostage to privately owned banks as was the case in the UK banking collapse.

Q. That could cause chaos. Would you expect the nationalised banks to continue participation in the UK payment clearance system?

A. You are now asking further hypothetical questions based upon another hypothetical question involving potential commercial negotiations. Suffice to repeat that no new IS government would be held hostage to private banking interests.

Q. So you have no answer to this question?

A. Only a comment. The banking system has repeatedly caused economic and social chaos. It confronts democratic government at every turn considering itself above the law and accountable to no one but its own interests. The UK has lost this battle, but the Scots could withdraw in good order to another battlefield of their own choosing, just as they did at Bannockburn. This time it is not the English we fight but their bankers, and once again the strategy is confidential.

This is evidenced by the nature of these questions and responses. An IS will not be held hostage to its banking system.

3. Gold

A carry trade where you borrow and pay interest in order to buy something else that has higher interest. The gold carry trade works as follows. A central bank loans a bank (sometimes called a bullion bank) some gold. The gold lease rate is usually very low. The bullion bank immediately sells the gold and invests in securities with a higher rate of return, such as government long-term bonds.

The carry return is the return on the bonds minus the gold lease rate. However, this trade is risky on two dimensions. First, if the bullion bank invested in long-term bonds and the interest rate goes up, the trade could be unprofitable. More seriously, the bullion bank has effectively sold the gold short. If the loan is called by the central bank, and if gold has risen in value, the bullion bank will have to go into the market and purchase higher priced gold. Indeed, if many banks are short, the unwinding of the gold carry trade could drive the gold price even higher.

'New Dictionary of Money & Investing'. C.R. Harvey.

Reprinted from GATA- a civil rights and educational organization based in the United States.

While central banks traditionally have said they lease gold to earn a little money on a supposedly dead asset, in 1998 Federal Reserve Chairman Alan Greenspan told Congress that this was not true. Central banks lease gold, Greenspan admitted, to suppress its price:

For years prior to 2000, gold leasing fuelled what was called the gold carry trade. Investment houses leased gold from central banks, paying the central banks a tiny annual interest rate, usually well below 1 percent of the value of the gold leased, and then sold the gold into the market and invested the proceeds in government bonds, earning perhaps 5 percent annually. The huge difference in interest rates meant a virtually free stream of income for the investment houses, income paid by central banks as interest on the government bonds purchased by the investment houses, secure as long as the investment houses could be protected against sudden rises in the price of gold.

Gold-leasing governments liked this scheme because it supported government bond prices and government currencies, and kept interest rates down - below where a free market would have set them. The results were the worldwide, credit-fuelled boom, a vast misallocation of capital into unprofitable, unsustainable enterprises, and the worldwide bust now under way.

When the price of gold reached bottom in 1999, and turned up threatening the investment houses that had sold leased gold even as western central bank gold reserves began to decline markedly, the western european central banks, under the supervision of the U.S. government, announced the Central Bank Gold Agreement:

The U.S. government was not formally a signatory to the agreement, but it was announced in Washington and has been called the Washington Agreement. So it is fairly surmised that the U.S. government helped organize the agreement and had a big interest in it - the continuing support of the U.S. dollar and U.S. government bonds through gold price suppression. Gold price suppression was the essence of the "strong dollar policy." The Washington Agreement was a plan of dishoarding and sale of the gold reserves of the western european central banks.

While the agreement's participants said they meant to support the gold price by limiting and co-ordinating their gold dishoarding, in fact they were arranging cash settlement of their gold loans, allowing the investment houses that were short gold to close their positions in cash rather than in gold itself. The investment houses were allowed to settle in cash because if they had been required to settle in gold, they would have had to go into the open market to get it, and the gold price would have shot up very high, bankrupting the investment houses and greatly diminishing the value of all government currencies and bonds.

That is, central banks do not want their leased gold back. That is what you are missing.

Ever since the Washington Agreement in 1999, the western central banks have been managing their controlled retreat with the gold price, letting gold rise a fairly steady 15-20 percent per year on average, stretching out their dishoarding as far as they can while trying to maintain some gold on hand for emergency intervention in the currency markets.

Barrick Gold, the biggest hedger (short) among the gold miners, confirmed all this when it announced some years ago that most of its gold loans had 15-year terms and were what the company called 'evergreen' - always allowed to be rolled over year after year so that the gold never had to be repaid as long as Barrick paid the tiny amount of cash interest due on it every year. Barrick is short more than 9 million ounces of gold and until a few years ago was short much more than that. Who would lend so much gold indefinitely and for a mere pittance in interest? Only a central bank that meant to suppress gold as part of a scheme to keep government currencies and government bonds up and interest rates down.

Defending against Blanchard Co.'s gold price-fixing lawsuit in U.S. District Court in New Orleans in 2003, Barrick went so far as to claim to be the agent of the central banks when it leased and sold gold and to share their sovereign immunity against lawsuit: That is, gold is only the tail on the dog here. But it's a very strong tail.

More details about the gold price suppression scheme can be found by reference to the following:-

http://www.gata.org.

http://www.federalreserve.gov/boarddocs/testimony/1998/19980724.htm

http://www.reserveasset.gold.org/central_bank_agreements/cbga1

4. Privatisations

1970s: British Petroleum); International Computers Limited; Lunn Poly; Rolls-Royce Motors; State Management Scheme; Thomas Cook .

1980s Amersham International; Associated British Ports; British Aerospace; British Airports Authority; British Airways; British Airways Helicopters; British Gas; British Leyland ; Alvis; Coventry Climax ; Danish Automobile Building ; Istel; Jaguar; Leyland Bus; Leyland Tractors; Leyland Trucks; Rover Group; Unipart; British Rail Engineering Limited; British Shipbuilders British Steel; British Sugar ; British Telecom; British Transport Hotels; Britoil; Cable and Wireless ; Council Houses (1980–present, over two million sold to their tenants); Enterprise Oil; Fairey Aviation; Ferranti; Inmos ; Municipal Bus Companies; National Bus Company; National Express; National Freight Corporation ; Passenger Transport Executive Bus Companies; Rolls-Royce; Royal Ordnance; Sealink; Trustee Savings Bank; Anglian Water; Northumbrian Water; North West Water ; Severn Trent; Southern Water; South West Water; Thames Water; Welsh Water; Wessex Water; Yorkshire Water;

1990s: 3G Spectrum; AEA Technology; Agricultural Development and Advisory Service ; Belfast International Airport ; Birmingham Airport; Bournemouth Airport; Bristol Airport; British Coal ; British Energy; British Rail; Angel Trains; Eversholt Leasing; Porterbrook; 6 Design Office Units; Freightliner; Loadhaul ; Mainline Freight; Rail Express Systems; Railfreight Distribution; Transrail Freight; Infrastructure Maintenance Units; 25 Train Operating Companies; British Rail Research; British Rail Telecommunications; European Passenger Services; Railtrack – no Network Rail; Red Star Parcels; Union

Railways; British Technology Group; Building Research Establishment; Cardiff Airport; Central Electricity Generating Board; National Grid; National Power; Powergen; Chessington Computer Centre; National Savings; East Midlands Airport; Girobank; Humberside Airport; Kingston Communications; Laboratory of the Government Chemist; Liverpool Airport; London Buses; London Luton Airport; London Southend Airport; National Engineering Laboratory; National Transcommunications Limited; Natural Resources Institute; Northern Ireland Electricity; Property Services Agency; Eastern Electricity; East Midlands Electricity; London Electricity; MANWEB; Midlands Electricity; Northern Electric; NORWEB; SEEBOARD; Southern Electric ; SWALEC; SWEB Energy; Yorkshire Electricity; Scottish Bus Group; Scottish Hydro-Electric; Scottish Power; Severn Bridge; Student loans portfolio; The Stationery Office; Transport Research Laboratory;

2000s: Trust Ports; Actis; BBC Technology; British Nuclear Fuels Limited; AWE Management Limited; Directory Enquiries; BNG America; BNG Project Services; Reactor Sites Management Company; Westinghouse Electric Company; East Thames Buses; Leeds Bradford International Airport; National Air Traffic Services; Newcastle Airport; Partnerships UK; Qinetiq; Teesside International Airport; UKAEA Limited; 4G spectrum ; Fire Service College; High Speed 1 ; Manchester Airports Group; Northern Rock; The Tote.

Most of these original assets named here are now difficult to trace having been bought & sold in the free market in the UK and abroad. Of over 150 odd privatisations, ten from the FTSE 2013 are valued at over £220 bn.

5. The Sterling Area or Zone

The Sterling Area ceased to exist in 1980 with the adoption of floating exchange rates. Crown Dependencies of Channel Islands, and British Overseas Territories like Gibraltar and the Falkland Islands use sterling. Most are required to lodge sterling assets with the Bank of England to back their cash – as with Scottish banknotes – but all are pegged to the pound sterling, and are expressions of identity and of no economic significance.

The Manx Currency Act 1992 binds the Isle of Man Treasury to exchange Manx banknotes for sterling upon demand, in practice accepting the same limitations on the issue.

In passing there is some £5.2bn worth of Scottish banknotes in circulation and even a Scots pound issued on the Isle of Man pattern would bring no public benefit. It would release this sum back to the banks but as this is a deposit in any case it is already 'their' money.

There is no point in adopting any sterling based currency because that still leaves the fractional reserve banking system in control of the economy.

BIBLIOGRAPHY

Common Weal Reid Foundation Library (2013)

ONS: Office of National Statistics Westminster Gov Publication

GERS: Government Expenditure & Revenues Scotland Westminster Government Publication.

"An Inquiry into the nature and causes of the Wealth of Nations" Adam Smith (1775)

'Marx & Engels Selected Works' Lawrence & Wishart (1968)

'The General Theory of Employment, Interest and Money' John Maynard Keynes (1936)

'A History of the Scottish People 1560-1830' T.C. Smout Fontana (1969)

Liberal Party leaflet 'We can conquer unemployment' Lloyd George (1929)

'Principles of Economics' Alfred Marshall (1886)

Scotland on Sunday Newspaper article by Alistair Darling MP (Feb: 2013)

'Freefall' Joseph Stiglitz (2010) Penguin books

'A history of British Trade Unionism' Henry Pelling (1963) Pelican Books.

'Capitalism and Freedom' Milton Friedman University of Chicago Press

'Road to Serfdom' Friedrich Hayek (1944) amazon

Minutes of the Labour Party Conference (1976)

'Leadership & Democracy' Stephen Williams & R.H. Fryer (2011) Lawrence & Wishart.

'The Politics of the UCS Work-In' John Foster & Charles Woolfson (1986) Lawrence & Wishart

The McCrone Report Scottish Office (1974) Top Secret

The Holyrood Magazine (May 2013)

'Gordon Brown' Tom Bower, Harper Perennial.

'Mismanagement of Britain' Dr Jim Cuthbert, Reid Foundation Library (2013)

'Has Scotland already spent its oil fund?' Professor Brian Ashcroft (2013)

'The Healers: A history of Medicine in Scotland' David Hamilton (1981) Canongate Publishing Ltd

'Creating New Money' Joseph Huber & James Robertson, New Economics Foundation (2000)

'Positive Money' www.positivemoney.org.

'The Grip of Death' Michael Rowbotham (1998)

'The Money Bomb' James Gibb Stuart (1984)

www.LeftFootForward.org

INDEX

INDEX

Note: Any specific page may contain multiple references to the indicated item.

A

B

C

D

E

F

G

H

I

J

K

L

M

N

O

P

R

S

T

INDEX